Practice Games for
WINNING
SOCCER

Practice Games for WINNING SOCCER

J. Malcolm Simon
John A. Reeves

Editors

Human Kinetics

Library of Congress Cataloging-in-Publication Data

Practice games for winning soccer / J. Malcolm Simon, John A. Reeves, editors.

    p. cm.
    ISBN 0-88011-631-5
    1. Soccer--Training. I. Simon, J. Malcolm. II. Reeves, John A. (John Albert), 1939-
    GV943.9.T7P73 1997
    796.334'2--dc21

97-2612
CIP

ISBN: 0-88011-631-5

This book is a revised edition of *The Soccer Games Book,* published in 1982 by Human Kinetics Publishers, Inc.

Photos on pages vi and xvi appear courtesy of UCLA Sports Information. Photo on page xiv appears courtesy of University of Connecticut Sports Information. Photo on page 82 appears courtesy of Fresno State Sports Information.

Acquisitions Editor: Ken Mange; **Developmental Editor:** Kent Reel; **Assistant Editors:** Jennifer Stallard and Tony Callihan; **Editorial Assistant:** Jennifer Hemphill; **Copyeditor:** Denelle Eknes; **Proofreader:** Tom Long; **Graphic Designer:** Stuart Cartwright; **Graphic Artist:** Tom Roberts; **Photo Editor:** Boyd LaFoon; **Cover Designer:** Jack Davis; **Photographer(cover):** Stock Market / Mark Gamba; **Illustrator:** Sara Wolfsmith; **Printer:** United Graphics.

Human Kinetics books are available at special discounts for bulk purchases. Special editions or book excerpts can also be created to specification. For details, contact the Special Sales Manager at Human Kinetics.

Printed in the United States of America   10 9 8 7 6 5 4 3 2 1

Human Kinetics
Web site: http://www.humankinetics.com/

United States: Human Kinetics
P.O. Box 5076, Champaign, IL 61825-5076
1-800-747-4457
e-mail: humank@hkusa.com

Canada: Human Kinetics
Box 24040, Windsor, ON N8Y 4Y9
1-800-465-7301 (in Canada only)
e-mail: humank@hkcanada.com

Europe: Human Kinetics
P.O. Box IW14,
Leeds LS16 6TR, United Kingdom
(44) 1132 781708
e-mail: humank@hkeurope.com

Australia: Human Kinetics
57A Price Avenue, Lower Mitcham,
South Australia 5062
(08) 277 1555
e-mail: humank@hkaustralia.com

New Zealand: Human Kinetics
P.O. Box 105-231, Auckland 1
(09) 523 3462
e-mail: humank@hknewz.com

DEDICATION

To the coaches who contributed to one or more of our books: *The Coaches Collection of Soccer Drills*, *The Soccer Games Book*, *Select Soccer Drills*, *Soccer Restart Plays*, and *Practice Games for Winning Soccer*. Through their professional dedication and willingness to share their knowledge, the sport of soccer continues to improve.

CONTENTS

Part II Games That Teach Tactics and Teamwork   83

PREFACE

It is generally accepted that athletes learn better when having fun. This is not to say that only activities that athletes typically enjoy a great deal, such as scrimmage games, will result in significant learning. There are times when the coach will realize that his or her players are just going through the motions of drills without any significant learning taking place.

We cannot overemphasize the importance of drills. We illustrate our appreciation of this importance in our books, *The Coaches Collection of Soccer Drills, Select Soccer Drills,* and *Soccer Restart Plays.* However, constant drilling can be boring and ineffective, as can inordinately relying on scrimmaging. There is a viable alternative to drilling and scrimmaging—the use of soccer-related games. Soccer-related games are useful in coaching soccer. Games that emphasize soccer techniques, tactics, and fitness add variety to practice sessions, keeping them interesting, enjoyable, and productive. Although useful for all ages, games are particularly helpful in coaching the young player with a short attention span. Regardless of the player's age and level of ability, interest remains high and the learning response improves in an atmosphere of enjoyable competition.

To be effective games should meet certain objectives:

- They should have purpose or emphasis.
- They should allow for repetition of action, particularly in the technique or tactic being emphasized.
- They should call for some measure of control or accuracy.
- They should simulate game conditions.
- They should be fun.

The games included in *Practice Games for Winning Soccer* meet these objectives. In addition to a few of our favorite games, *Practice Games for Winning Soccer* includes games that successful high school and college coaches throughout the United States have contributed.

We have divided the book into two parts. Part I includes games that emphasize skills. Part II includes games that teach tactics and teamwork. The book's Game Finder makes it easy for the coach to locate games with specific emphases. Most of the games have more than one emphasis, and some emphasize both skills and tactics. For games with more than one emphasis, we have listed them in the order that the authors and editors want to stress. In some games the designation of emphasis or emphases is not hard and fast, and the coach can determine which emphasis or emphases fit his or her team's needs for a particular practice session. Coaches can adapt all games to the players' abilities by varying the size of the area, number of players, types of passes, and number of touches permitted.

We have arranged the games alphabetically within each part and clearly illustrated them. The written description and diagram of each game include the information necessary to effectively organize the games. Directly after the name of each game and its contributor are the emphasis or emphases, recommended number of players, and equipment needed. Following this information are a setup section, the description of the game, and, finally, game variations, if any. The setup section will describe the recommended playing area and how the players are organized within the area. The description of the game will explain the object of the game, exactly how it is played, and some coaching tips. The variation section will include recommendations for making the game easier or more difficult, or how to vary the game's emphasis. This information, with the diagram of the game, will make it easy for the coach to understand and select the game or games appropriate for practice sessions.

CONTRIBUTING AUTHORS

CONTRIBUTOR	INSTITUTION
Michael Alosco	Manhattan College, Riverdale, NY 10471
John A. Astudillo	University of Buffalo, Buffalo, NY 14260
Tom Breznitsky	Scotch Plains Fanwood High School, Scotch Plains, NJ 07076
Candy Canzoneri	Otterbein College, Westerville, OH 43081
Pete Caringi	University of Maryland-Baltimore County, Baltimore, MD 21236
Rob Chesney	Montclair State University, Upper Montclair, NJ 07043
Gene Chyzowych	Columbia High School, Maplewood, NJ 07040
Gus Constantine	New York Institute of Technology Old Westbury, NY 11568
Michael A. Costa	Jackson Memorial High School, Jackson, NJ 08527
Andrew Crawford	Hilbert College, Hamburg, NY 14075
Michael Coven	Brandeis University, Waltham, MA 02254
Helio D'Anna	Union College, Barbourville, KY 40906
Brian Dooley	Barry University, Miami Shores, FL 33161
Betsy Duerksen	University of Montana, Missoula, MT 59801
B. Todd Dyer	Longwood College, Farmville, VA 23909
Jim Felix	Buckingham, Browne, and Nichols School, Cambridge, MA 02138
Cheri L. Goetcheus	Swarthmore College, Swarthmore, PA 19081
Barry Gorman	Pennsylvania State University, University Park, PA 16802
Nelson Graham	Wayne Soccer Club, Wayne, NJ 07470
Terrence Gurnett	University of Rochester, Rochester, NY 14627
Colleen Hacker	Pacific Lutheran University, Tacoma, WA 98447
Dan Kilday	New Jersey Institute of Technology, Newark, NJ 07102
TJ Kostecky	Pfeiffer University, Misenheimer, NC 28109
Steve Locker	Harvard University, Cambridge, MA 02138
Andrew Lowery	Sparta High School, Sparta, NJ 07871
Joseph A. Luxbacher	University of Pittsburgh, Pittsburgh, PA 15241

CONTRIBUTOR

INSTITUTION

CONTRIBUTOR	INSTITUTION
Joseph A. Machnik	Major Soccer League
Denis Mayer	Piscataway High School, Piscataway, NJ 08854
Kevin McCarthy	Columbia University, New York, NY 10027
William J. McGrath	Caldwell College, Caldwell, NJ 07006
Debbie Michael	International Soccer Academy, Austin, TX 78734
Michael Mooney	SUNY at Geneseo, Geneseo, NY 14454
Michelle Morgan	Amherst College, Amherst, MA 01002
Jerry Moyer	Moravian College, Bethlehem, PA 18018
Nick Mykulak	Stevens Institute of Technology, Hoboken, NJ 07030
Fran O'Leary	Dartmouth College, Hanover, NH 03755
Mike Pilger	University of Rochester, Rochester, NY 14627
Tracey Ranieri	SUNY at Oneonta, Oneonta, NY 13802
John A. Reeves	Columbia University, New York, NY 10027
Fred Schmalz	University of Evansville, Evansville, IN 47722
Rob Searl	St. John Fisher College, Rochester, NY 14618
J. Malcolm Simon	New Jersey Institute of Technology, Newark, NJ 07102
Matthew Smith	Johns Hopkins University, Baltimore, MD 21239
Stephen J. Swanson	Stanford University, Stanford, CA 94305
Tom Taylor	Hawthorne High School, Hawthorne, NJ 07506
Jeff Tipping	Muhlenberg College, Allentown, PA 18104
Susan Viscomi	SUNY at Oswego, Oswego, NY 13136
Kendall Walkes	West Chester University, West Chester, PA 19383
Tim Wheaton	Harvard University, Cambridge, MA 02138
Brian Woods	William Paterson College, Wayne, NJ 07470
Richard Zawacki	Don Bosco Prep High School, Ramsey, NJ 07446

GAME FINDER

Emphasis	Game Number
Attack	44, 46, 47, 49, 51, 54, 57, 58, 59, 60, 64, 65, 66, 69, 71, 72, 73, 75, 76, 79, 80
Clearing	3, 7, 23
Communication	41, 50, 52, 55, 78
Defense	10, 11, 33, 44, 46, 47, 48, 49, 50, 51, 54, 56, 57, 58, 59, 60, 63, 64, 65, 66, 68, 69, 70, 71, 73, 75, 76, 79
Dribbling	9, 11, 12, 17, 18, 25, 27
Fitness	9, 10, 12, 17, 18, 22, 24, 28, 29, 37, 41, 46, 52, 53, 60, 67, 78
Goalkeeping	4, 15, 24, 26, 31, 32, 36, 37, 39, 46, 58, 69
Heading	1, 7, 16, 23, 78
Juggling	17, 41
Movement off the Ball	3, 41, 42, 53, 70
Passing	4, 5, 8, 10, 12, 13, 14, 16, 20, 21, 22, 23, 29, 30, 33, 35, 40, 41, 42, 43, 44, 61, 72, 74
Possession	12, 43, 45, 53, 61, 63, 67, 70, 72, 74, 77
Receiving	5, 22, 40
Shooting	1, 2, 3, 4, 6, 7, 8, 13, 14, 19, 20, 23, 24, 26, 27, 28, 29, 31, 32, 33, 34, 35, 36, 37, 38, 39, 42, 43, 68, 69, 72
Transition Play	21, 34, 50, 55, 57, 62, 65, 68, 74, 76, 79

KEY TO DIAGRAMS

⚽	Ball
🔺	Cone
◯	Disc cone
– – – – –→	Pass
∿∿∿→	Dribble
──────→	Run
· · · · · ·→	Shot
X	Field player
A	Attacker
D	Defender
G	Goalkeeper
C	Coach
F	Feeder (or Flank player)
R	Retriever
N	Neutral player
B	Bumper
S	Server (or Saver)
J	Juggler
CM	Central midfielder
OM	Outside midfielder

PART ONE

GAMES FOR INTENSIVE SKILL PRACTICE

It is essential for soccer players to learn the basic soccer skills before being introduced to tactics. The sooner players master the critical skills of dribbling, heading, passing, receiving, and shooting, the sooner they will be able to comprehend tactics. Using games that emphasize one or two skills is the quickest way for players to learn or master these skills. In determining which games to use in practice, consider the ability levels of the players. Introduce neophyte players to simple games emphasizing preferably one and no more than two skills without any defensive pressure. Young players need to be successful in handling the basics before moving to more challenging situations that could involve decision-making opportunities. As the players' ability levels increase, the coach can introduce games that are more physically and mentally challenging. Such games might involve one or more challenges, for example, defensive pressure, space and time limitations, speed of repetition, and ballhandling restrictions.

Games will also improve the players' fitness under fun and competitive conditions. Relays, for example, can emphasize a specific skill such as dribbling or juggling, while the pressure of completing the relay within a time limit can achieve the same fitness benefits.

The games in this part, arranged alphabetically by title, will emphasize clearing, dribbling, goalkeeping, heading, juggling, passing (including chipping and crossing), receiving, and shooting (including finishing and penalty kicking).

Air Soccer

1

Contributors: Editors

Emphases: Heading, shooting

No. of Players: 8

Equipment Needed: 1 ball, 4 cones, 2 goals, 8 practice jerseys

Setup: Two teams of four players each spread out within a 20-by-20-yard area bordered by a cone at each corner. Each team wears different-colored practice jerseys. An indoor-size goal is at the midpoint of opposite end lines. A player on one team has a ball.

Directions: The player with the ball starts the game with a toss to a teammate. The game is 4 v 4 with the ball always played in the air. The team loses ball possession to the opponents when the ball touches the ground or is intercepted in the air. Shots on goal must be head or foot volley shots and may be taken from anywhere. The team ahead after a set time, or the first team to score a set number of goals, is the winner.

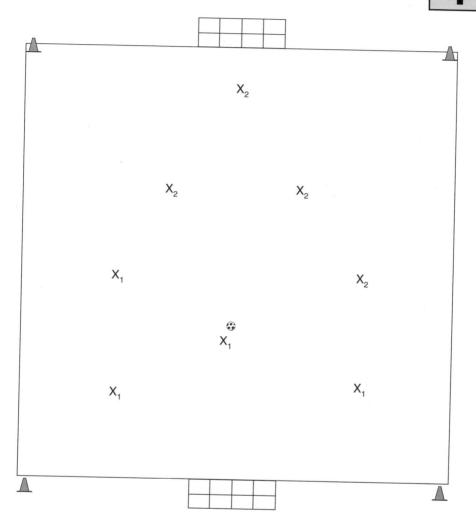

Back-to-Back Goals

2

Contributor: Tim Wheaton, Harvard University

Emphasis: Shooting

No. of Players: 22

Equipment Needed: 6 balls, 6 cones, 2 goals, 20 practice jerseys

Setup: The game is played in a 40-by-40-yard area using the midfield line of a regulation field to divide the area into two playing areas. The area is marked by a cone at each corner and each sideline at midfield. Two goals are placed back to back at the midpoint of the midfield line. Two teams of 10 players each wear different-colored practice jerseys. Five players from each team are within the area in front of each goal. A goalkeeper is in each goal. The coach, with six balls, stands at midfield outside the area.

Directions: The coach begins play with a pass into the middle of one playing area. The teams battle for possession, after which they play 5 v 5 and try to score on either goal. The players must stay in their own area but may pass the ball across midfield to a teammate. A missed shot on goal that crosses midfield is kept in play by the team in that area who gains possession of the ball. A goalkeeper making a save throws the ball anywhere into the opposite playing area. The coach passes another ball into any playing area following a goal or ball going over any sideline or end line. The team first scoring a predetermined number of goals wins.

Variations:

1. Goals must be scored only by head shots.
2. Restrict players to one touch.

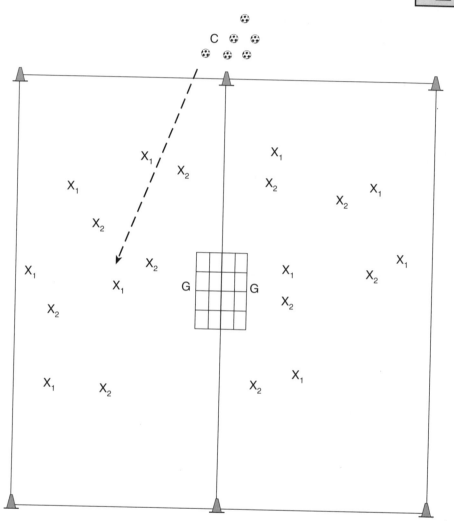

Bok Wars

Contributor: Stephen J. Swanson, Stanford University

Emphases: Shooting, clearing, movement off the ball

No. of Players: 17

Equipment Needed: 8 balls, 1 goal, 16 practice jerseys

Setup: The game is played in the penalty area. There are two teams of eight players each. Each team wears different-colored practice jerseys. The coach designates one team as attackers and the other as defenders. Four attackers and four defenders are positioned within the penalty area. Four other attackers are positioned outside the penalty area—one outside each sideline and one on each side of the penalty area restraining arc. The other four defenders are behind the goal and serve as ball shaggers. A goalkeeper is in goal. The coach, with a supply of balls, is within the penalty area restraining arc.

Directions: The coach starts play by either passing the ball to one of the attackers within the penalty area or passing it to one of the attackers outside either sideline. The object of the game is for the attackers to score and for the defenders to clear balls out of the penalty area. The attackers within the area may shoot at any time or play the ball back to one of the attackers on either side of the restraining arc. This attacker must take a first-time shot on goal. The two sideline attackers are permitted two touches to cross the ball into the penalty area. Attackers within the box must be aware of each other's runs so they do not cover the same spots or clog the area. The defenders must stay with the players they are marking until the ball is cleared. After every goal, clearance, or out-of-bounds play, the coach sends in another ball. Play is continuous for a predetermined time of two to five minutes, after which the teams rotate responsibilities. Each goal or clearance counts one point. The team with the most points wins.

Variations:

1. Use fewer players within the area (2 v 2 or 3 v 3) to allow more room for players to move.

2. Goals scored from crosses on first time count two points.

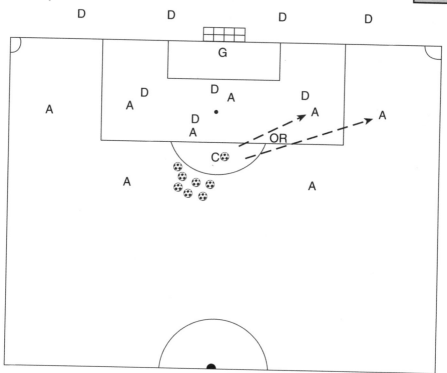

Bombardment

Contributor: Cheri L. Goetcheus, Swarthmore College

Emphases: Shooting, passing, goalkeeping

No. of Players: 7

Equipment Needed: 12 balls, 1 goal

Setup: The game is played in one-half of a soccer field. Three teams of two players each, X1, X2, and X3, are located respectively at the center of the midfield line and each sideline at a point even with the top of the penalty area line. A goalkeeper is in goal. The coach stands behind the goal. The sideline players, goalkeeper, and coach each has three balls.

Directions: The game starts with a punt or throw from the goalkeeper to the X1s at midfield (1). They control the ball and dribble and pass between them toward goal with one player shooting on goal from outside the penalty area (2). Immediately after the shot, an X2 crosses the ball toward the top of the penalty area for an X1 to shoot first time on goal (3). The X2s then sprint to the midfield area vacated by the X1s (4). Following the cross from X2, an X3 makes a similar cross for an X1 to make a first-time shot on goal (5). The X3s then sprint across the field to the area vacated by the X2s (6). Following the cross by X3, the coach serves a ball from behind the goal for an X1 to take a first-time head shot on goal (7). The X1s then sprint to the sideline area vacated by the X3s (8). The X1s must alternate shots on goal. Play restarts with a punt or throw from the goalkeeper to the X2s. Each goal counts one point. The game continues until each team has had three opportunities to be attackers. The team with the most goals wins.

Variations:

1. Add two defenders.
2. Specify the spot where the crosses are to be made.

Bombardment

4

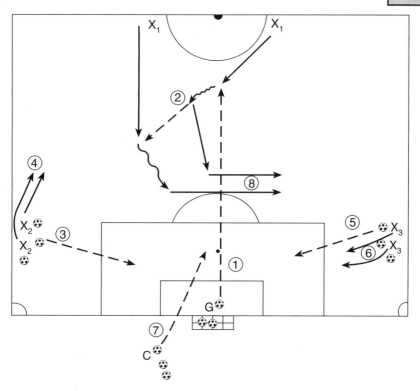

5 Brazilian Passing Game

Contributor: Jeff Tipping, Muhlenberg College

Emphases: Passing, receiving

No. of Players: 16

Equipment Needed: 1 ball, 16 upright cones, 35 disc cones, 16 practice jerseys

Setup: The game is played in an area 70 yards long by 48 yards wide, divided by disc cones into four vertical corridors, each 12 yards wide by 70 yards long. A goal, marked by two cones four yards apart, is at the end line of each corridor. There are two teams of eight players each, wearing different-colored practice jerseys. Two players from each team are within each corridor. A player from one team has a ball.

Directions: The teams play 8 v 8, with 2 v 2 in each corridor. The player with the ball starts play with a pass to a teammate in a different corridor. Players must stay in their own corridor but cannot pass in their own corridor. The object of the game is to score in any of the four goals. Following a goal, a player on the team scored upon restarts play with a pass to a teammate in a different corridor. Play is continuous for 20 minutes. The team with the most goals wins. The coach emphasizes the following points: 1. Pass diagonally. 2. If a teammate is marked, pass the ball to the foot away from the marker. If teammate is free, pass the ball to the foot closest to the opponent's goal. 3. Supporting players position themselves sideways to see peripherally and receive passes sideways as the Brazilians do.

Variation: Players can move into different corridors but still cannot pass the ball in the same corridor.

Brazilian Passing Game

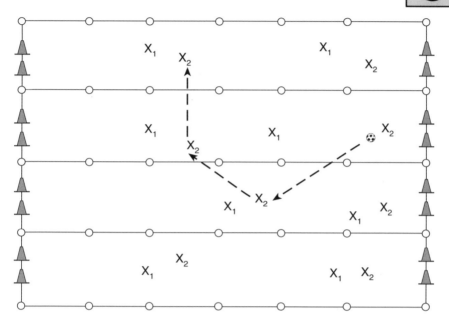

5

Circle to Shoot

6

Contributors: Editors

Emphasis: Shooting

No. of Players: 22

Equipment Needed: 10 balls, 1 cone, 1 goal

Setup: The game is played in one-quarter of the field including the penalty area. There are two teams of 10 players each. One team lines up behind the goal. The other team spreads out behind the end line and around the penalty area and serves as retrievers. A feeder is just outside the penalty area restraining arc. Ten balls are near the feeder. A cone is placed five yards past the feeder. A goalkeeper is in goal.

Directions: The team behind the goal begins running, each player leaving some space between the next player, in a large circle from one goalpost, around the cone, and back behind the opposite goalpost. After passing the cone, each shooter receives a pass from the feeder and takes a first-time shot on goal. After two minutes, the teams change roles. The team scoring the most goals wins.

Variations:

1. The shooters make the circle run in the opposite direction and shoot with the other foot.

2. The feeder makes loft passes and the shooters take first-time volley shots on goal.

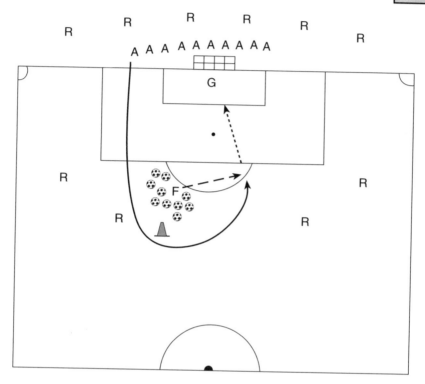

7 Clear Them Out

Contributors: Editors
Emphases: Clearing, heading, shooting
No. of Players: 12
Equipment Needed: 12 balls, 1 goal

Setup: The game is played in one-quarter of a field including the penalty area. There are two teams of six players each. One team spreads out within the penalty area. The other six players, each with two balls, stand in different positions about 10 yards outside the penalty area.

Directions: The attackers alternate chipping balls into the penalty area in an attempt to score. The defenders try to prevent balls from entering the goal or landing in the penalty area by clearing or heading balls out of the area. Points are scored as follows: three points for a goal, two points for a ball touching the ground in the goal area, and one point for a ball touching the ground in the remainder of the penalty area. After 12 shots, the teams change roles. The team scoring the most points wins.

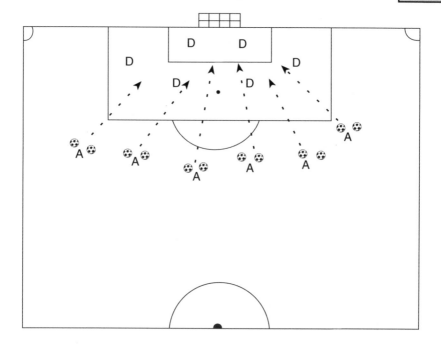

8 | Competitive Crossing and Shooting

Contributor: Barry Gorman, Pennsylvania State University

Emphases: Passing, shooting

No. of Players: 18

Equipment Needed: 16 balls, 2 goals

Setup: There are two groups of nine players each. Each group is positioned in and around the penalty areas of the soccer field as shown in the diagram. Each group includes a goalkeeper. X1, X3, X4, and X7 each has a ball. X8 has an extra supply of balls. X5 and X6 stand behind the end line to shag balls and return them to X8 at appropriate times.

Directions: In each penalty area, X1 starts play with a give-and-go with X2. X1 takes a first-time shot on goal after the return pass from X2. Following the shot on goal, X1 and X2 continue toward the goal to receive and shoot on goal a serve from X4. X1 and X2 have a combined total of two touches (i.e., either player can shoot first time, control and shoot, or pass to the other player who takes the shot). Any rebounds off the goalkeeper or crossbars give X1 and X2 another two touches to finish the play. Once they complete that play, X7 serves to X1 and X2 for a similar opportunity to score. Players then rotate positions as follows: X1 to X2 to X3 to X4 to X5 to X6 to X7 to X8 to X1. Play continues until each player has been in all positions. The group scoring the most goals wins.

Variations:

1. Have X4 and X7 dribble to the end line and cross balls from that spot.

2. Add a defender, D1, behind X2 and follow same game directions. Players rotate X1 to X2 to D1 to X3, and so on.

3. Add two defenders, D1 and D2, in the goal area to defend against crosses. Players rotate X1 to X2 to X3 to X4 to X5 to D1 to D2 to X6 to X7 to X8 to X1.

Competitive Crossing and Shooting

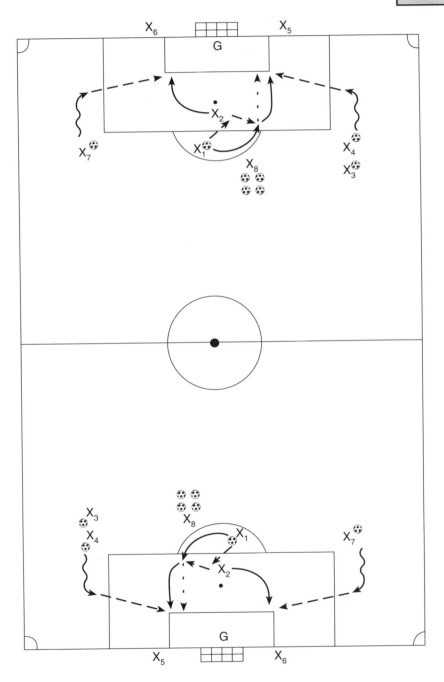

Dribble Relay

Contributors: Editors

Emphases: Dribbling, fitness

No. of Players: 6 to 12

Equipment Needed: 2 balls, 12 cones

Setup: Two teams of equal numbers line up in relay fashion on one sideline and face a course 30 yards long. Cones are placed at five-yard intervals in front of the starting line for each team.

Directions: One player from each team begins running the course at a signal from the coach. The players dribble as fast as possible to the first cone and back to the starting line. The players then go to each of the next cones and back to the starting line each time until they complete the course. After a player finishes the course, the next player goes until each player completes the course. The team completing the course first is the winner.

Variations:

1. Time each player's run, creating competition between players and motivation to achieve personal best times.

2. Have the players circle each cone before returning to the starting line.

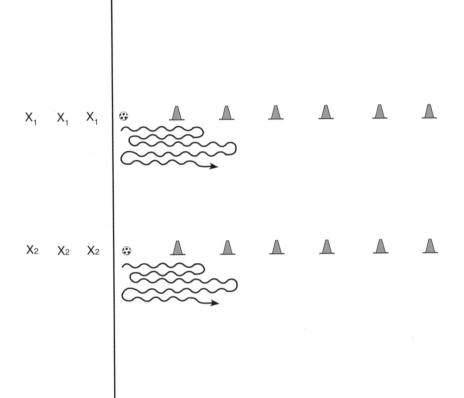

Dynamic Keep-Away

Contributor: Helio D'Anna, Union College

Emphases: Passing, defense, fitness

No. of Players: 10

Equipment Needed: 2 balls, 8 cones

Setup: Two 10-by-10-yard grids, 8 yards apart, are bordered by a cone at each corner. Ten players are grouped into five pairs. Two pairs are in each grid—X1 and X2 in grid 1, and X3 and X4 in grid 2. The fifth pair, X5, is in the area between the grids. One player in each grid has a ball.

Directions: The game starts on a signal from the coach. The X5 players sprint to grid 1. The X1 and X2 players in that grid attempt to complete 10 consecutive passes, while the X5s attempt to intercept the ball or force it out of the grid. If 10 consecutive passes are completed, the X5s sprint to grid 2 where the X3 and X4 players have started passing the ball. The counting of the passes begins as soon as the 10 passes were made in grid 1. If the X5s steal the ball or force it out-of-bounds, the player to last touch the ball and his or her partner become defenders and sprint to grid 2. Play is continuous until one pair completes 10 passes four times. Players should count passes aloud. The coach emphasizes constant movement, encouraging players not to stand still.

Variations:

1. Have only one defender and play 4 v 1.
2. Restrict passes to two or one touch.
3. Do not allow passes back to the player who made the last pass.

Grid 1

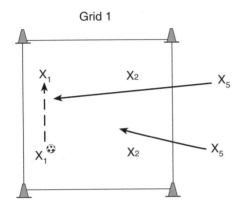

Grid 2

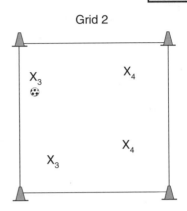

End All

Contributor: Tom Breznitsky, Scotch Plains Fanwood High School

Emphases: Dribbling, defense

No. of Players: 10

Equipment Needed: 8 balls, 4 cones, 2 practice jerseys

Setup: Ten players are positioned within an area 15 yards wide by 20 yards long bordered by a cone at each corner. Eight attackers, each with a ball, line up along one end line. Two defenders are positioned at the midpoint of the area.

Directions: The eight attackers use a full range of dribbling skills to beat the two defenders to reach the opposite end line. The defenders are allowed to move laterally only. If the attackers are tackled or lose possession of the ball, they join the defenders. If they reach the opposite end line, they turn and attempt to beat the defenders in the opposite direction. Play is continuous until one attacker remains. This player is the winner.

Variations:

1. Attackers may use only the left or right feet in dribbling.

2. Attackers must use a specific move to beat the defenders.

3. Defenders may move in any direction.

4. Increase the number of defenders.

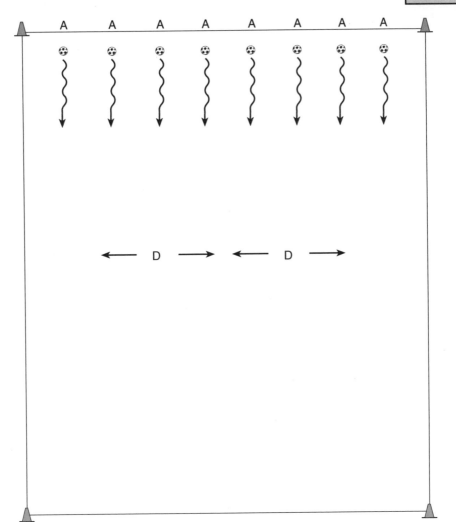

Epitok Hungarian Box

Contributor: Rob Searl, St. John Fisher College

Emphases: Dribbling, passing, possession, fitness

No. of Players: 10

Equipment Needed: 1 ball

Setup: The game is played in the goal area. Ten players spread around the perimeter of the area, with three players on each end line and two players on each sideline. Each player receives a number from 1 to 10. A ball is in the middle of the area. The coach stands outside the area.

Directions: The game starts when the coach calls out two numbers. The players with these numbers run into the box. Each player attempts to gain possession of the ball, after which the players play 1 v 1 for 45 seconds. The player in possession of the ball may use individual ball skills (dribbling, shielding, etc.) or use any of the perimeter players for one- or two-touch passes. After 45 seconds, the coach signals the end of play and calls out two new numbers. These players move to gain possession of the ball. The players on the field leave the ball where it was when the coach called time and move to the positions vacated by the new field players. The player in each pair who maintains ball possession the longest is the winner.

Variations:

1. To emphasize passing, award one point for each successful combination play between a field player and a perimeter player. The player with the most points in 45 seconds is the winner.

2. Play 2 v 2 in same area.

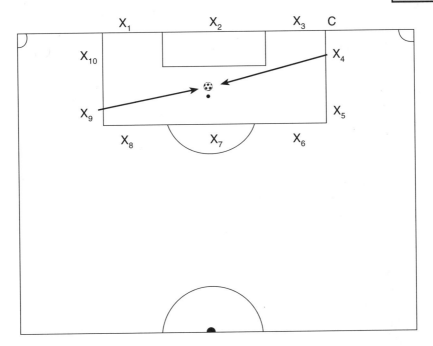

Everyone Shoots

Contributor: Tom Taylor, Hawthorne High School

Emphases: Shooting, passing

No. of Players: 12

Equipment Needed: 1 ball, 6 cones, 2 goals, 10 practice jerseys

Setup: The game is played in an area 20 yards wide by 40 yards long bordered by a cone at each corner. A cone is also placed at the midpoint of each sideline to divide the area into halves. A goal is at the midpoint of each end line. A goalkeeper is in each goal. There are two teams of five players each, one team wearing blue jerseys and the other red jerseys. Three blue and two red players are in one-half of the area, and three red and two blue players are in the other half. One of the red players has a ball.

Directions: This is a total shooting game with the players on each team shooting on the opposite goal. The red player with the ball starts play with a shot on goal or pass to a teammate. The three red players attempt to shoot on the opposite goal or pass the ball to either of the two red players in the opposite half of the area, who attempt a shot on the goal behind the three red players. The blue players in each half attempt to gain possession of the ball and attack in the same fashion as the red players. The players are restricted to their respective half of the area. Out-of-bounds balls are put back in play by a pass from a player on the team not causing the ball to go out-of-bounds. Goals and goal saves are put back in play by a pass from the goalkeeper to a player on the opposite team. Play is continuous for 20 minutes. The team scoring the most goals wins.

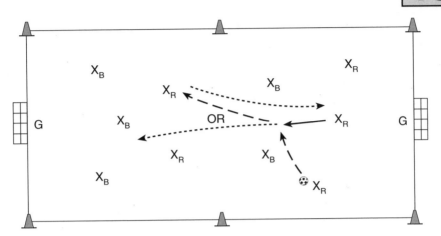

Finishing Game

Contributor: Denis Mayer, Piscataway High School

Emphases: Shooting, passing

No. of Players: 20

Equipment Needed: 12 balls, 12 cones, 2 goals, 18 practice jerseys

Setup: The game is played in the penalty area. A shooting area is defined within the penalty area by using cones to extend the sidelines of the goal area to the 18-yard line. There are two groups of 10 players each, wearing different-colored practice jerseys. Each group is split into three teams of three players and one goalkeeper. Three players from each team are located within the shooting area. Three other players from each team spread along opposite sidelines of the penalty area. These players are the crossers and have two balls each. The remaining three players from each team spread outside opposite end lines. These players are the chasers and keep the crossers supplied with balls. A goal is at the midpoint of each end line. A goalkeeper is in each goal.

Directions: On a signal from the coach, the crossers alternately serve balls to the shooters on their team, who take first-time shots on the opponent's goal. This continues until one team scores three goals. When this occurs, the players on each group switch roles until all three teams have been shooters. The group making the most goals wins.

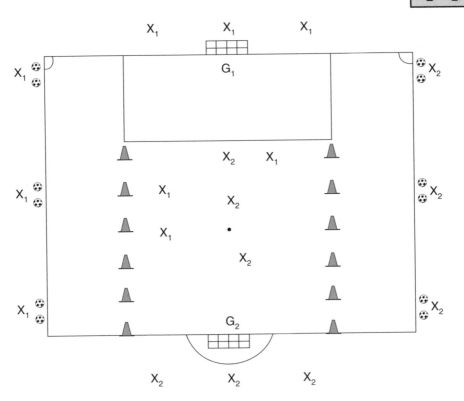

Goal Sweeping

Contributor: Joseph A. Machnik, Major Soccer League

Emphasis: Goalkeeping

No. of Players: 8

Equipment Needed: 1 ball, 14 cones, 2 goals

Setup: The game is played in part of one-half of a soccer field. The sidelines of the penalty area are extended to midfield by using cones to mark the width of the playing area. The midfield line of the playing area is marked by a cone at the midpoint of each sideline. A goal is at the midpoint of the end line and another one is at the midpoint of the midfield line. There are two teams of three players each, wearing different-colored practice jerseys. Each team is within its respective half of the area. A goalkeeper is in each goal. The coach, with a ball, stands outside the midpoint of the area.

Directions: The coach starts a 3 v 3 game with a pass to a player on either team. The object of the game is to encourage the goalkeeper to handle offside traps, through passes, breakaways, and other *crisis* situations. The goalkeeper may only use his or her hands inside the goal area or center circle at midfield to play the opponent's shots, but may not use hands outside these areas or at any time on passes from teammates. A point is awarded for each goal scored and each time the goalkeeper forces the opponents to lose possession of the ball. Play is continuous for 20 minutes. The team with the most points wins.

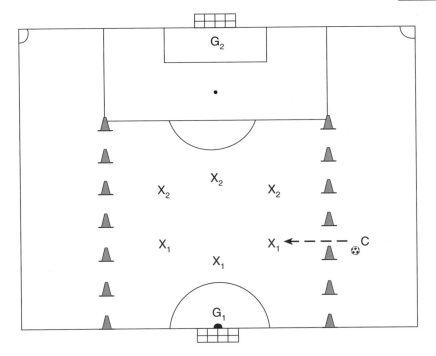

Headers and Crosses

Contributors: Editors

Emphases: Heading, passing

No. of Players: 13

Equipment Needed: 5 balls, 1 goal

Setup: The game is played in the penalty area. There are two teams, X1 and X2, of six players each. An X1 player, with five balls, is located at the midpoint of one sideline of the penalty area. The other X1 players are in a line just outside the goal area opposite the player with the balls. The X2 players stand behind the goal to retrieve balls. A goalkeeper is in goal.

Directions: Each X1 player takes turns at serving crosses to each of the other X1s, who alternate taking first-time head shots on goal. After each player has had a turn at crossing the balls, the teams change roles. Points are scored as follows: two points for each goal scored, one point for each shot that requires a goal save, no points for any shot off target, minus one point for any cross that cannot be headed. The team with the most points after each team has completed one round is the winner.

Variation: Make crosses from both sides of the penalty area.

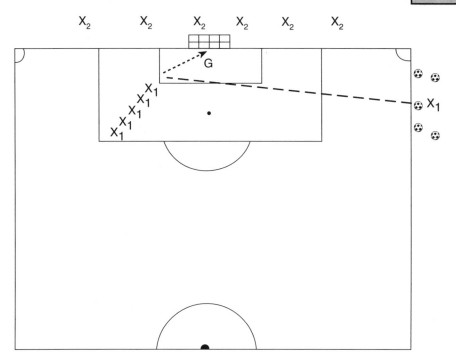

Juggling Relay

17

Contributors: Editors

Emphases: Juggling, dribbling, fitness

No. of Players: 8 or more

Equipment Needed: 1 ball per team

Setup: The relay is run from one sideline to the opposite sideline. Two or more teams of four players each line up five yards apart from each other on one sideline. The first player in each line has a ball.

Directions: On a signal from the coach, the first player in each line begins executing a set number of juggles. After completing the juggling, each player dribbles at top speed to the opposite sideline, picks up the ball, sprints back to the starting line, and hands the ball to the next player in line, who repeats the routine. The team completing the relay first is the winner.

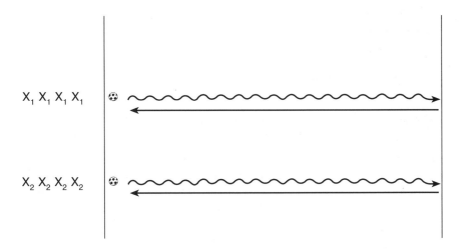

$X_1 \, X_1 \, X_1 \, X_1$

$X_2 \, X_2 \, X_2 \, X_2$

Kick Them Out

18

Contributors: Editors

Emphases: Dribbling, fitness

No. of Players: 6

Equipment Needed: 6 balls

Setup: Two teams of three players each are within the center circle. Each player has a ball.

Directions: On a signal from the coach, all players dribble within the circle. While dribbling, the players on each team try to kick the opponent's balls out of the circle. The team that kicks all the opponent's balls out first is the winner.

Variations:

1. Increase the number of players.
2. Play individually. The last player in the circle wins.

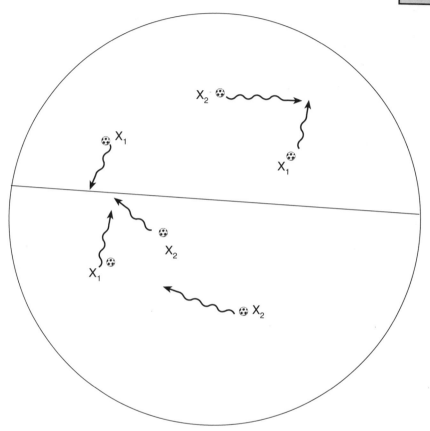

King of the Goal

19

Contributor: Pete Caringi, University of Maryland-Baltimore County

Emphasis: Shooting

No. of Players: 6

Equipment Needed: 12 balls, 2 goals

Setup: Two goals are located 20 yards opposite each other. A goalkeeper is in each goal. Two players, X1 and X2, stand facing each other in front of opposite goals. Twelve balls are placed in a line midway between the goals. Another player is behind each goal to retrieve balls.

Directions: On a signal, each player begins taking shots on the opposite goal at the same time. The object is to shoot as quickly and accurately as possible. The player who scores the most goals wins. One of the retrievers comes on to challenge the winner.

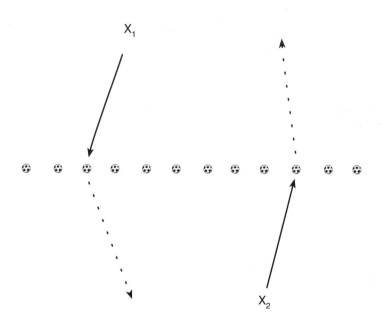

Long Shots

Contributors: Editors

Emphases: Shooting, passing

No. of Players: 10

Equipment Needed: 1 ball, 6 cones, 2 goals

Setup: The game is played in a 40-by-40-yard area bordered by a cone at each corner and opposite sidelines at midfield. There are two teams of five players each. Four players from each team spread out within their respective half of the area. A player on one team has a ball. A goal is at the midpoint of opposite end lines. A goalkeeper is in each goal.

Directions: This is a 5 v 5 game, but players must stay in their own half and set up to take long shots on the opponent's goal. Players use one or two touch. After each shot on goal, the goalkeeper passes the ball to a teammate. The team with the most goals after a set time wins.

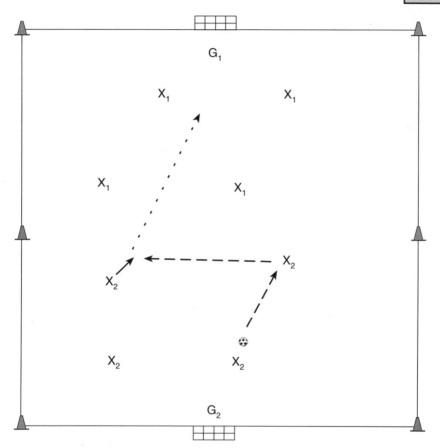

Moving Three Versus One

Contributor: Tom Taylor, Hawthorne High School

Emphases: Passing, transition play

No. of Players: 6

Equipment Needed: 1 ball, 8 cones

Setup: The game is played in two 8-by-8-yard grids positioned 30 yards from each other. Both grids are bordered by a cone at each corner. Four players, three attackers and one defender, are in one grid. One of the attackers has a ball. The remaining two players are in the other grid.

Directions: At a signal from the coach, the players in the first grid play a 3 v 1 game. After five consecutive passes, the player receiving the fifth pass kicks a long pass in the air to the two players in the other grid. As the ball is kicked, the other two players on the passing team sprint to the second grid. The long ball kicker and the defender stay in the first grid. The player who loses the sprint to the second grid now plays defense in another 3 v 1 game. Play continues in this fashion for 20 minutes.

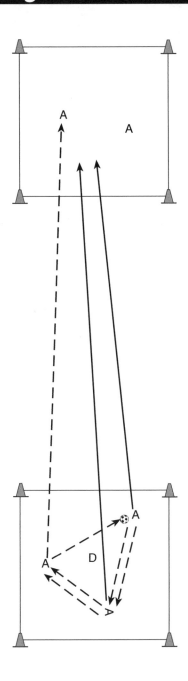

Multiple Goals Game

Contributor: William J. McGrath, Caldwell College

Emphases: Passing, receiving, fitness

No. of Players: 10 to 20

Equipment Needed: 1 ball, 14 cones, 10 to 20 practice jerseys

---

Setup: The game is played in a 40-by-40-yard area bordered by a cone at each corner. Five goals are randomly positioned within the area. Each goal is two yards wide and marked by two cones. Two teams of 5 to 10 players each, wearing different-colored practice jerseys, are located within the area. A player on one team has a ball.

Directions: The object of the game is for the player with the ball to pass it through a goal and have it received by a teammate. A point is scored each time this occurs. Play is continuous until one team scores seven points. The team without the ball attempts to gain possession. If a team intercepts the ball and scores a point, the opponents lose their accumulated points. If the team that lost possession regains the ball before a point is scored, they keep all their points. The team that scores seven points first wins.

Variations:

1. For younger players, increase size of area and goals.
2. For advanced players, limit touches for each player.

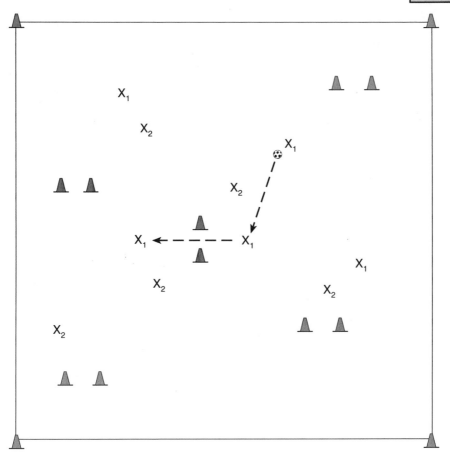

23 Open Goal

Contributor: Richard Zawacki, Don Bosco Prep High School

Emphases: Clearing, heading, passing, shooting

No. of Players: 16

Equipment Needed: 1 ball, 20 disc cones, 2 goals, 16 practice jerseys

Setup: The game is played in one-half of a soccer field using the goal line and midfield line as end lines. An indoor-size goal is at the midpoint of each end line. A flank area along each sideline is designated by setting 10 disc cones at equal intervals, five yards inside each sideline from goal line to midfield line. There are two teams of eight players each, X1 and X2, wearing different-colored practice jerseys. Two players from each team spread along the flank areas. Four players from each team are positioned within their respective half of the playing area. A player on the X1 team has a ball. Flank players may move anywhere along their flank area but may not enter the playing area. Field players may move anywhere within the field but may not enter either flank area. There are no goalkeepers.

Directions: The game starts with a pass from the X1 player with the ball to any field or flank teammate. Following the pass the field players play 4 v 4, with the X1s attacking the opposite goal while the X2s attempt to gain possession of the ball and move on attack. Goals may be scored only by a cross from a flank player to a field player who must take a first-time head or volley shot on goal. Defenders attempt to head or clear the ball out of play or to a teammate. A ball going out-of-bounds is put back in play by a free pass from a player on the team not causing the ball to go out-of-bounds. Play is continuous for 20 minutes with the field and flank players switching positions at 10 minutes. The team with the most goals at the end of play is the winner.

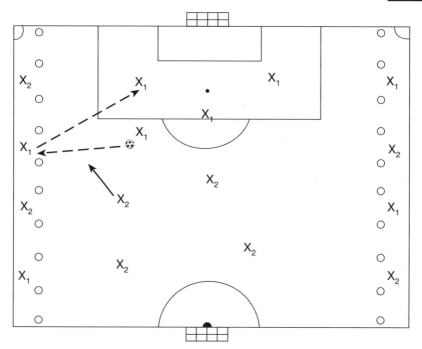

Penalty Kick Conditioning Game

24

> **Contributor:** Brian Woods, William Paterson College
>
> **Emphases:** Shooting, goalkeeping, fitness
>
> **No. of Players:** 15
>
> **Equipment Needed:** 7 balls, 5 cones, 1 goal

Setup: The game is played in one-half of a soccer field. There are two teams of seven players each. One team stands along the penalty line. The other team stands behind the goal to retrieve balls. A supply of balls is located in the penalty area restraining arc. A goalkeeper is in goal. Five cones are placed at 5-yard intervals extending 25 yards from the top of the penalty area.

Directions: The shooting players take turns shooting penalty kicks until each player has taken two shots. If any player shoots high or wide, the entire team sprints from the penalty line to the line marked by the first cone, back to the penalty line, and continues sprinting back and forth to all five cone lines. After one team has completed a round, the teams switch positions and the other team shoots a round of penalty kicks. The team scoring the most penalty kicks after one or more rounds is the winner.

Penalty Kick Conditioning Game

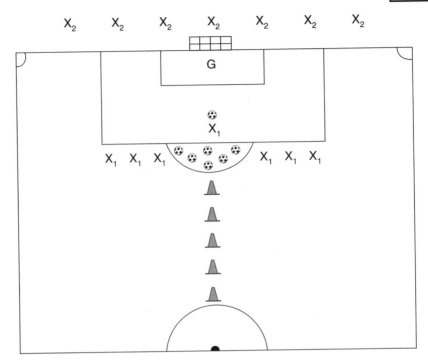

25 Pinball

Contributor: William J. McGrath, Caldwell College

Emphasis: Dribbling

No. of Players: 10 to 20

Equipment Needed: 5 to 10 balls, 4 cones

Setup: The game is played in a 25-by-25-yard area bordered by a cone at each corner. Two teams of 5 to 10 players each are located within the area. The players on one team are the *bumpers* and sit on the ground with their legs crossed close to the body. Each player on the other team has a ball.

Directions: The players with the balls dribble within the area. The bumpers attempt to knock the balls away from the dribblers. The bumpers must remain seated and use only their hands to knock the balls away. They may not catch the ball. A dribbler can regain the ball and continue dribbling. After three minutes the teams switch roles. The team knocking away the most balls wins.

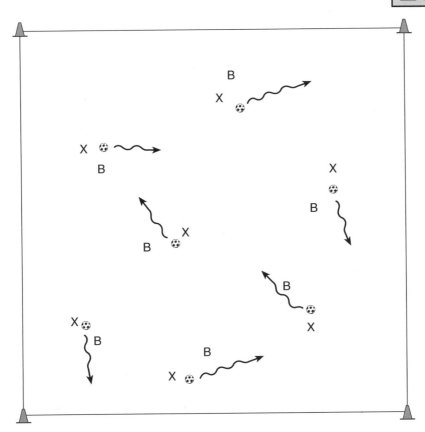

Shooting Contests

Contributor: Pete Caringi, University of Maryland-Baltimore County

Emphases: Shooting, goalkeeping

No. of Players: 10

Equipment Needed: Supply of balls, 2 cones, 1 goal

Setup: The games are played in the penalty area. There are two teams of four players each. Each team is in a column behind the end line of opposite goalposts. A cone is on the penalty area line directly opposite each team. Two goalkeepers are in goal, each one near the opposite post. In games 1 and 3, the first player in each line has the ball. In games 2 and 4, the second player in each line has the ball.

A supply of balls is outside each goalpost.

Directions: The teams will compete at the same time in a series of four shooting games. In game 1, each player alternately dribbles a ball around the team's cone and shoots on goal. In game 2, each player alternately runs without a ball around the cone, back to the six-yard line, and heads on goal a ball served by the next player in line. In game 3, each player alternately runs with a ball around the cone and takes a volley shot on goal out of the shooter's hand. In game 4, each player alternately runs around the cone and shoots an air volley shot on goal from a chip pass made by the next player in line. The team making the most goals wins. If the score is tied, the teams take alternate penalty kicks against alternating goalkeepers until one team wins.

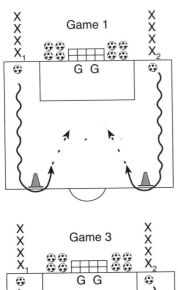

Game 1

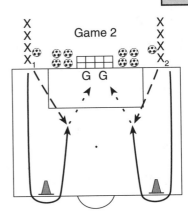

Game 2

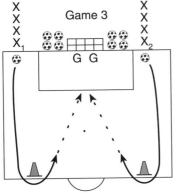

Game 3

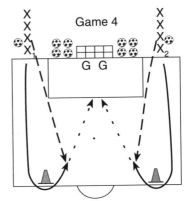

Game 4

Side Net

Contributor: Kendall Walkes, West Chester University

Emphases: Shooting, dribbling

No. of Players: 3 to 6

Equipment Needed: 1 ball, a supply of cones, 1 goal

Setup: The game is played within the penalty area. Cones are placed one yard outside the side and top lines of the penalty area at five-yard intervals to form a perimeter boundary. Three players, X1, X2, and X3, are within the penalty area. A coach, with a ball, stands in the penalty area restraining arc.

Directions: The coach starts play with a pass to X1. X1 tries to score against the defense of X2 and X3. A goal is scored only when the ball enters the triangular side net area of the goal. The game is played with the same ball possession as half-court basketball. Whenever one of the defenders gains possession of the ball, that player must dribble the ball outside the perimeter of the penalty area within the boundary line before attacking on goal. The two players without the ball go immediately on defense when they lose ball possession. Play is continuous for 10 minutes. The player with the most goals wins.

Variation: Play with three teams of two players each.

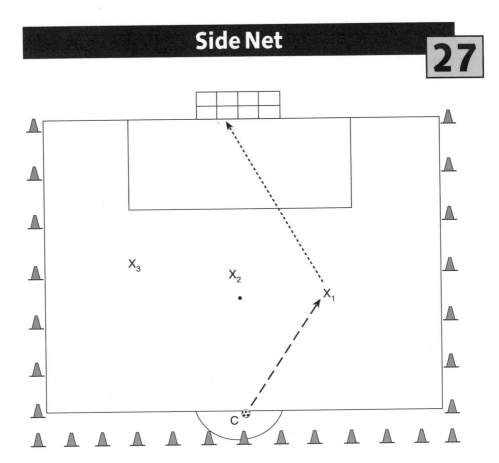

Soccer Fire Away

Contributor: Pete Caringi, University of Maryland-Baltimore County

Emphases: Shooting, fitness

No. of Players: 8

Equipment Needed: 20 balls, 4 cones, 4 goals

Setup: The game is played in a 40-by-40-yard grid bordered by a cone at each corner. A goal is at the midpoint of each sideline. Twenty balls are distributed within the grid. There are two teams of four players each. Two players from each team are located within the grid. Each other player is at a different corner of the grid.

Directions: At a signal, each pair of players competes against the other at the same time to shoot the balls within the grid at any of the four goals. After each shot on goal, the shooters must sprint to touch any of the corner players before taking another shot on goal. Shooting continues for 45 seconds after which the shooters change roles with the corner players. The group of four players scoring the most goals wins.

Variations:

1. Only one player from each team is in the grid.
2. Decrease the size of the grid for less conditioned players.
3. Add defenders.

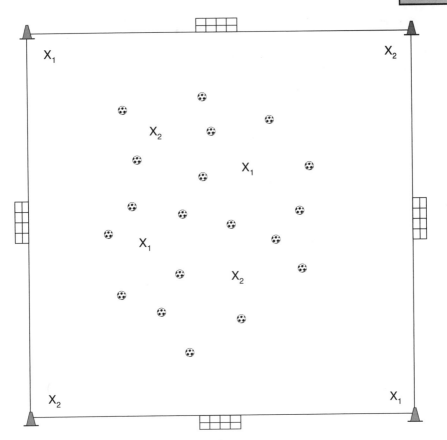

Soccer Wall

Contributor: Nick Mykulak, Stevens Institute of Technology

Emphases: Passing, shooting, fitness

No. of Players: 2

Equipment Needed: 1 ball (soccer or volleyball)

Setup: The game is played in a four-wall racquetball or squash court, or a single-wall paddleball court. Two players, X1 and X2, are positioned within the court. X1, with a ball, is within the service area. X2 is within the receiving area.

Directions: X1 starts play with a volley kick past the service line to X2. X2 must kick the ball back to the front wall before the ball bounces twice. Any returned ball may hit a side wall and then hit the front wall. X1 and X2 alternate kicking the ball until it bounces twice or does not hit the front wall on the fly. A ball hitting the ceiling is out of play. Points are scored only when serving. The first player to reach 15 points and have at least 2 points more than his or her opponent is the winner.

Variations:

1. Require different serves (e.g., instep, inside or outside of foot air volley, chip from floor, or left or right foot only).

2. Require different returns (e.g., left or right foot only, direct to front wall with no side wall touch allowed, before one bounce for advanced players, and before three bounces for beginners).

3. Require control of ball before returning ball to wall.

4. Play 2 v 2 or 2 v 1 (cutthroat).

Safety Note: Stress to the players to be aware of not running into the walls.

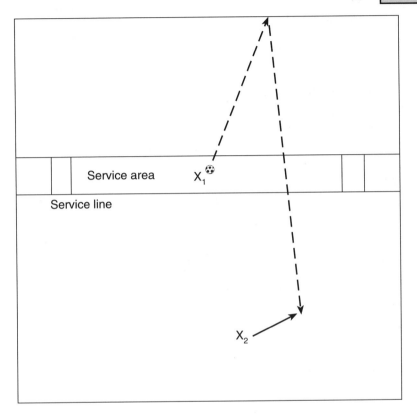

Service area X₁

Service line

X₂

Target Ball

30

Contributors: Editors

Emphasis: Passing

No. of Players: 14

Equipment Needed: 11 balls

Setup: The game is played in the penalty area. Two teams of seven players face each other on opposite end lines. One player from each team is within the penalty area. Each team has four balls. Three target balls, a different color from the team balls, are in the center of the area.

Directions: On a signal from the coach, each team kicks their balls in an attempt to drive the target balls across the opponent's end line. Each team's player in the area fields balls and returns them to his or her teammates. Players may move along either sideline of the area but may not cross the opponents' end line. Players may not interfere with an opponent's play or kick the target ball. The first team to kick the target balls across the opponent's end line wins.

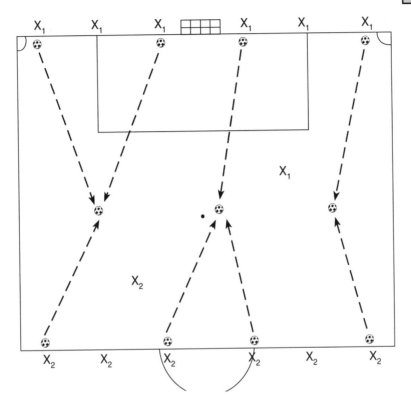

31

Contributor: Colleen Hacker, Pacific Lutheran University

Emphases: Shooting, goalkeeping

No. of Players: 12

Equipment Needed: 3 balls, 1 goal, 1 stopwatch

Setup: The game is played in one-half field. A goal is at the midpoint of the end line. Three teams of three players each, A1, A2, and A3, are in three lines at midfield. A player on each team has a ball. A goalkeeper is in goal. Two other goalkeepers are behind the goal.

Directions: The A1 team begins an attack by passing or dribbling toward goal. The attackers must score a goal in no more than 30 seconds. The attackers must take the first shot outside the penalty area. If the shot goes in, the coach records the time. If the shot misses, the attackers must retrieve the ball and continue their attempt to score within 30 seconds. If the goalkeeper saves the shot, the goalkeeper immediately rolls the ball out anywhere within the penalty area where the attackers must retrieve it and continue their attempt to score. If time expires before a goal is scored, play ends and the attackers must sprint back to midfield. Following a goal or expiration of time, the next team begins their attack on goal. A new goalkeeper moves in goal each time the three teams complete their attacks. The coach keeps a record of the time each team scores a goal and the shutouts for each goalkeeper. After a predetermined time or number of attacks, the team scoring a goal in the fastest time and the goalkeeper with the most shutouts are the winners.

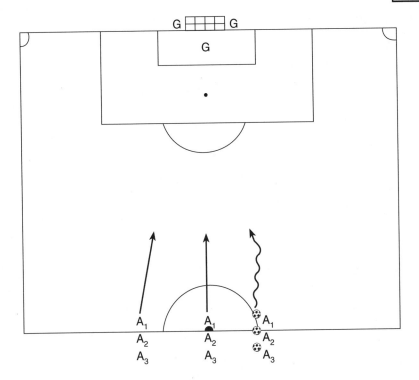

32

Three-Point Shooting

Contributor: Steve Locker, Harvard University

Emphases: Shooting, goalkeeping

No. of Players: 5

Equipment Needed: 9 balls, 1 goal

Setup: The game is played in an area 40 yards from the goal including the penalty area. A goal is at the midpoint of the end line. A goalkeeper is in goal. There are two teams of two players each, X1 and X2. Two X1s, each with a ball, stand in a line 40 yards from the goal. Two X2s, each with a ball, are in a line five yards to the side of one goalpost. A coach, with five balls, stands five yards to the side of the opposite goalpost.

Directions: One X1 dribbles toward goal (1) and takes a shot on goal from outside the penalty area (2). As soon as X1 takes the shot, one X2 passes a ball to X1 just inside the penalty area (3) for X1 to take a first-time shot on goal (4). As soon as X1 takes this shot, the coach makes an air pass just outside the goal area (5) for X1 to take a first-time head shot on goal (6). Play continues in this fashion until each X1 has taken three rounds of shots. After this, the X1s and X2s switch roles. The team scoring the most goals after three rounds each is the winner.

Variation: Instead of team competition, have all players on attack, with a neutral feeder making the first pass followed by the coach's pass. The player making the most goals after a set number of rounds is the winner.

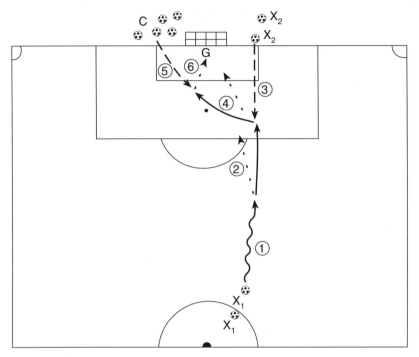

Three Versus One in Penalty Area

Contributor: Steve Locker, Harvard University

Emphases: Shooting, passing, defense

No. of Players: 6

Equipment Needed: 6 balls, 1 goal

Setup: The game is played in the penalty area. Three attackers and one defender are within the area. A goalkeeper is in goal. A server, with six balls, stands outside the penalty area restraining arc.

Directions: The server starts play with a pass to an attacker. The three attackers play one-touch soccer in an attempt to beat the defender and score a goal. If the shooter scores, the defender stays on defense. A shooter failing to score switches roles with the defender. An attacker making a bad pass or being the last player to touch a ball intercepted by the defender switches roles with the defender. Play stops after a shot on goal or change of possession and is restarted by a pass from the server. The player spending the least amount of time on defense is the winner.

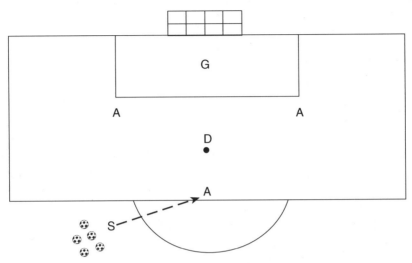

33

Three Versus Three Continuous

Contributor: Terrence Gurnett, University of Rochester

Emphases: Shooting, transition play

No. of Players: 20

Equipment Needed: 6 balls, 4 cones, 2 goals, 18 practice jerseys

Setup: The game is played in a 30-by-30-yard area bordered by a cone at each corner. A goal is at the midpoint of opposite end lines. There are two teams of 10 players each. Each team consists of three groups of three field players and one goalkeeper. Each team's field players wear different-colored practice jerseys. Three players from each team are positioned within opposite halves of the area. A player on one team has a ball. A goalkeeper is in each goal. The other two groups from each team are located behind the end line on opposite sides of their goal. A player on each team has a ball.

Directions: The game starts with a pass from the player with the ball to a teammate. The teams play 3 v 3 until a goal is scored or goes over the defensive end line. When this occurs, the defending team leaves the area and a new group enters the area and immediately attacks the other goal. A group stays on until they are scored upon or a ball goes over their end line. Balls going over the sideline are put back into play with a throw-in. Goalkeepers may not shoot on goal and may not use their hands on back passes from teammates. The coach should encourage the field players to shoot the ball at the first opportunity and the groups off the field to organize before their turn so they are ready to move onto attack immediately. Play is continuous for 20 minutes. The team with the most goals wins.

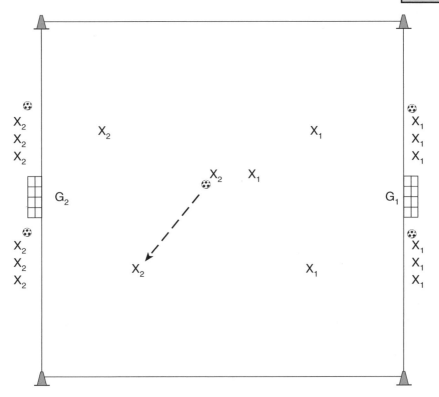

35 Three Zone Long-Range Shooting

Contributor: Jerry Moyer, Moravian College

Emphases: Shooting, passing

No. of Players: 10

Equipment Needed: 7 balls, 8 cones, 2 goals

Setup: The game is played in an area 45 yards long by 30 yards wide, which is divided into three zones of 18 yards, 9 yards, and 18 yards respectively. Cones mark the corners of the area and each zone. A goal is at the midpoint of each end line. There are two teams of five players each. Each team consists of three defenders, one attacker, and one goalkeeper. One attacker and three opposing defenders are in each 18-yard zone. The central 9-yard zone is unoccupied. A goalkeeper is in each goal. One goalkeeper has a ball. Extra balls are in each goal.

Directions: The game starts with a pass from the goalkeeper with the ball to any of the three defenders. The defenders may interpass within the zone but should pass the ball at the first opportunity to their attacker in the attacking zone. Although the attacker in the defensive zone tries to prevent the forward pass from the defenders, once the pass is made it cannot be intercepted by the defenders in the attacking zone. The target attacker plays the ball off to either of two teammates who have followed the initial pass into the central zone. A shot on goal must be taken at the first opportunity. One point is scored for each goal scored. If the defenders intercept the shot, the goalkeeper saves the shot, or the shot goes out-of-bounds, play continues in the opposite direction. Play is continuous for 20 minutes. The team with the most goals wins. The primary emphasis of the game is on shooting. The coach should encourage a positive attitude toward taking responsibility to shoot on goal at the first opportunity.

Variations:

1. Vary the number of players.
2. Shooters take first-time shots on goal.
3. Attackers must play ball to defender other than the one that made the forward pass.
4. Target attacker may turn and shoot on goal.

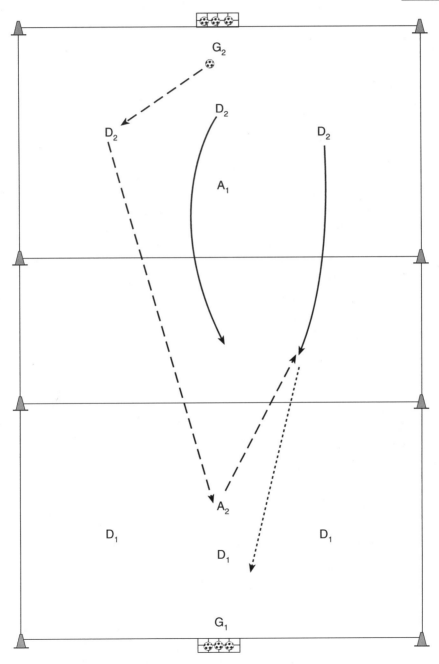

Trench

Contributor: Mike Pilger, University of Rochester

Emphases: Shooting, goalkeeping

No. of Players: 23

Equipment Needed: 12 balls, 4 upright cones, 8 disc cones, 2 goals

Setup: The game is played in a 35-by-35-yard area bordered by a cone at each corner. A goal is at the midpoint of each end line. Eight disc cones mark off a 4-by-15-yard trench in the middle of the area halfway between the goals. There are three teams of seven players each. Each team consists of five shooters and two trench players. One team spreads out behind opposite goals. The shooters from each of the other teams are positioned in opposite halves of the area. Two players from each of the other teams are positioned within the trench. A goalkeeper is in each goal. The coach, with 12 balls, stands at one side of the trench.

Directions: The coach begins play by serving a ball into the trench where the trench players battle for possession. The player gaining possession passes the ball to one of the shooters on the same team. The shooter takes a first-time shot on goal or makes a one-touch pass to a teammate who takes a first-time shot on goal. The opposing players try to block the shot. If an opposing shooter gains possession, he or she takes a shot on the opposite goal. If an opposing trench player gains possession, he or she passes to a shooter on the same team for a first-time shot on goal. The players behind the goals retrieve balls and return them to the coach. Immediately following a goal, goal save, or missed shot, the coach restarts play by serving another ball into the trench. The first team scoring two goals wins. The losing team is replaced by the team serving as retrievers. The team scoring the most goals after a predetermined time is the winner.

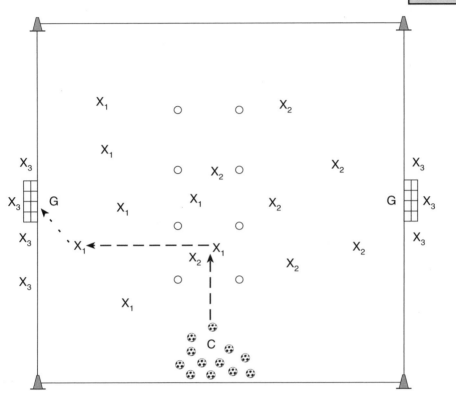

Contributor: Brian Woods, William Paterson College

Emphases: Shooting, goalkeeping, fitness

No. of Players: 15

Equipment Needed: 14 balls, 4 cones, 1 goal

Setup: The game is played in an area 25 yards from the end line of one-half field. There are two teams of seven players each. One team starts as the shooting team and stands along the 25-yard line, which is marked by four cones. The other team stands outside the end line to retrieve balls. Each player on the shooting team has a ball. Extra balls are located outside the 25-yard line.

Directions: On a signal from the coach, the shooting team players take turns shooting on goal for two minutes. A player shooting high or wide must sprint around the goal and back to the 25-yard line before shooting on goal again. After two minutes, the teams change places. The team with the most goals after one or more rounds of shots is the winner.

Variations:

1. Players take shots from a moving ball.
2. Introduce passive defenders to put some pressure on the shooters.
3. Increase the distance from the goal.
4. Shooters can follow up shots for possible rebound shots.

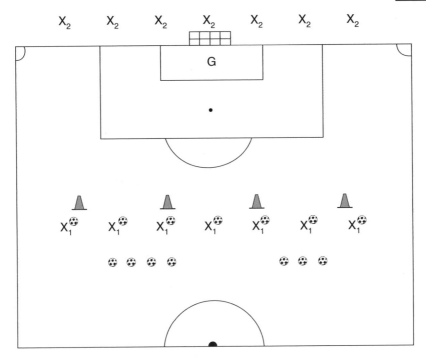

Contributor: Michael A. Costa, Jackson Memorial High School

Emphasis: Shooting

No. of Players: 14

Equipment Needed: 7 balls, 4 cones, 2 goals, 10 practice jerseys

Setup: The game is played in an area 25 yards long by 40 yards wide, bordered by a cone at each corner. A goal is at the midpoint of each end line. There are two teams of six players each, X1 and X2. Each team consists of five field players and one goalkeeper. The field players on each team wear different-colored practice jerseys. Each team is located within a different half of the area. A goalkeeper is in each goal. One of the X1s has a ball. Extra balls are in each goal. A feeder is located on each sideline midway between the goals.

Directions: The X1 player with the ball starts the game with a pass to a teammate or one of the feeders. The feeders may move along their respective sidelines but may not enter the playing area. The feeders receive passes and play balls to the team in possession of the ball. The X1s look to shoot at the earliest opportunity on the opposite goal. The X2s attempt to gain possession of the ball and go on attack. Out-of-bounds balls are put back in play by a pass from the goalkeeper on the team not causing the ball to go out-of-bounds. Play is restarted after a goal or goal save by a pass from the goalkeeper to a teammate. Play is continuous for 20 minutes. The team scoring the most goals wins.

Variations:

1. A field player may score a goal only by a first-time shot from a feeder's pass.

2. A field player may score a goal only by a head shot from a feeder's pass.

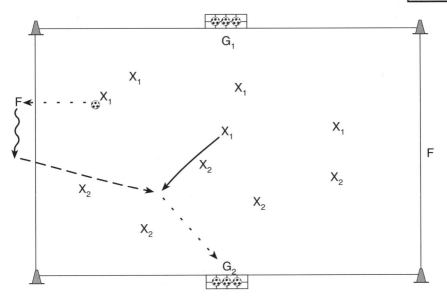

War Shooting

Contributor: Helio D'Anna, Union College

Emphases: Shooting, goalkeeping

No. of Players: 12

Equipment Needed: 6 balls, 2 cones, 1 goal

Setup: The game is played in the penalty area. A cone is set on the end line of each side of the goal, three yards from each goalpost. There are two teams of six players each. Each team has a goal-keeper. One team starts as shooters and stands in a vertical line just outside one side of the penalty area. Each player has a ball. A coach stands facing the shooters a few yards in front of them. The other team has a goalkeeper in goal, one saver by each goalpost, and three jugglers behind the goal.

Directions: The shooters will take shots on goal for three minutes. One player at a time will pass the ball to the coach, move to receive the return pass, and take a first-time shot on goal. The shooters do not wait for the goalkeeper to get set, but pass the ball to the coach as soon as each shot is taken. Each goal scored counts one point. The goalkeeper and savers try to save the shots on goal. The savers may not use their hands. Each time a goal is scored, the savers must sprint to the cones on their respective side and back to the goal area. The goalkeeper and savers try to send the ball over the goal to the jugglers, who try to control the ball before it hits the ground and keep it in the air by passing to each other. A point is scored for each successful pass. Points are scored until the ball hits the ground, after which the ball is left on the ground and the jugglers get ready for another air pass over the goal. The shooters retrieve their own balls but may not interfere with the players on the other team. If the jugglers are passing the ball in the air, the shooter must wait until the ball is dropped to retrieve it. Coaches or neutral players will keep score. After three minutes the teams switch places. The team with the most combined points after being on attack and defense wins.

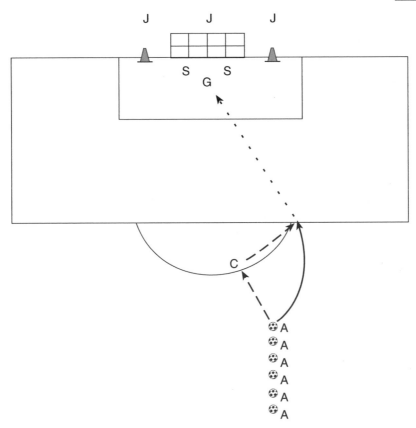

Who Has Best First Touch?

Contributor: TJ Kostecky, Pfeiffer University

Emphases: Passing, receiving

No. of Players: 2 to 4

Equipment Needed: 1 ball, 8 cones

Setup: The game takes place within two 4-by-4-yard grids that are 20 yards apart. Cones mark the borders of each grid. X1, with a ball, is in one grid, and X2 is in the other grid.

Directions: X1 begins the game by chipping the ball to X2. X2 must receive and control the ball within the grid and, on the second touch, chip the ball back to X1. If X2 does not control the ball within the grid, X1 receives one point. If either player does not serve the ball within the opposite grid, that player loses the serve and the opposite player receives one point. The game ends when one player receives 10 points.

Variation: Increase the grid size to six-by-six yards. Add an additional player to each grid. Play starts with a chip from either X1 player. The X2 player receiving the ball may control and pass the ball back immediately or may control and pass the ball to the other X2 player, who serves the ball back to opposite grid. Scoring remains the same.

PART TWO

GAMES THAT TEACH TACTICS AND TEAMWORK

As noted in the introduction to the skills part, players should not be introduced to tactics until they have achieved some ability in ballhandling skills. Although there is no fixed rule about when to introduce tactics, the coach should be aware of the critical relationship between skills and tactics, and know that good skills are essential to developing the soccer sense needed to make effective decisions in game situations.

Scrimmage-type games, from small sided to full team, can be easily adapted to stress tactics and, at the same time, improve ballhandling skills. As small-sided games give players more time with the ball than full-field scrimmages, using such games in practice will give the players more decision-making opportunities. The games in this part will expose players to tactics such as one-on-one situations, three or more players in combination play, and full-field work involving small groups up to full teams.

The games in this part, arranged alphabetically by title, will emphasize attack (including counterattack, exploiting a numerical advantage, one on one, penetration, support, and width), communication, defense (including handling a numerical disadvantage, marking, one on one, support, and zone), fitness, movement off the ball, possession (gaining and maintaining), and transition play.

Aerobic Soccer

Contributor: Debbie Michael, International Soccer Academy

Emphases: Communication, movement off the ball, fitness, passing, juggling

No. of Players: 6 to 30

Equipment Needed: 1 ball per group, stereo, dance music cassettes

Setup: The activity is held in a large, open area. The size of the area depends on the number of players, which can vary from 6 to 30 in groups of no more than 10 players each. A player in each group has a ball. A stereo is in one corner of the area. The music selected is dance music with a fast beat.

Directions: As the music starts, the players begin moving off the ball. The player with the ball calls out a player in the same group and passes the ball on the ground to that player. Passing continues in that fashion for five passes in a row. The player receiving the ball cannot return it to the player who passed it. On the sixth pass the player with the ball lifts it in the air and, after juggling it briefly, calls out a teammate and volley passes it to that player. Play continues in this fashion with the players attempting to keep the ball in the air for the duration of the activity, which can range from 20 to 30 minutes. The activity can be either competitive (more than one group) or noncompetitive (one group). If more than one group is involved, the group completing the most successive passes without error is the winner. In the competitive aspect, each time the ball touches the ground more than once while volley passing, the players must start play from the beginning. The coach emphasizes communication and enthusiasm throughout the activity and makes sure that players do not stand still and wait for a pass.

Variations:

1. Require each player to juggle the ball a specified number of times before passing it to another player.

2. More than one ball per group can be used.

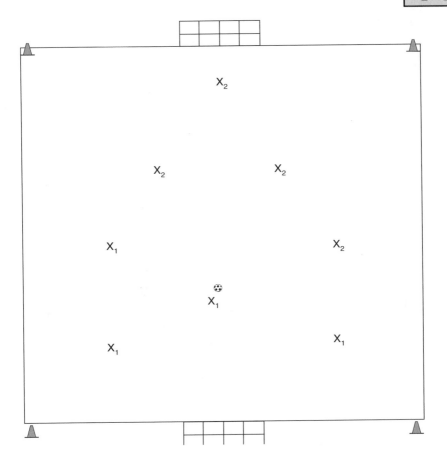

Don't Miss the Run

Contributor: John A. Astudillo, University of Buffalo

Emphases: Movement off the ball, passing, shooting

No. of Players: 16

Equipment Needed: 1 ball, 12 cones, 2 goals, 16 practice jerseys

Setup: The game is played in a full field divided into a playing area, a dead area, and a delivery area. The playing area is a 40-yard square in the center of the field. Surrounding the playing area is a 10-yard square dead area. Outside the dead area is the delivery area. A goal is at the midpoint of each end line. A goalkeeper is in each goal. Two teams of eight players each, X1 and X2, wearing different-colored practice jerseys, spread out within the playing area. One of the X1s has a ball.

Directions: The X1 with the ball starts play with a pass to a teammate (1). The X1s try to keep possession while the X2s attempt to gain possession of the ball. The players have a two-touch limit and must stay within the playing area. On the coach's direction, a player on the team with the ball makes an attacking run through the dead area into the delivery area (2). The player with the ball must recognize the run, make a pass into the delivery area to the player making the run (3), and follow the pass to support his or her teammate (4). If the run and pass are successful, the player receiving the ball takes a shot on goal or passes to the support player, who shoots on goal (5). If the run or pass is not successful, the ball goes to the other team, who attempts to make a successful run and pass in the opposite direction. Teams score a point for each successful run and pass, and for each goal scored. Play is continuous for a set time. The team scoring the most points wins.

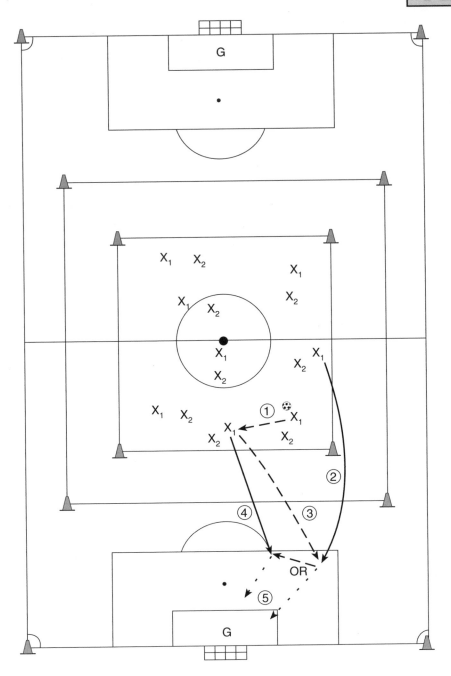

Eight Passes and Score

43

> **Contributor:** Michael Coven, Brandeis University
>
> **Emphases:** Possession, passing, shooting
>
> **No. of Players:** 12
>
> **Equipment Needed:** 1 ball, 2 goals, 10 practice jerseys

Setup: Two teams of five players each, wearing different-colored practice jerseys, are located within one-half of a soccer field. A goal is at the midpoint of the end line and midfield line. A goalkeeper is in each goal. One of the goalkeepers has a ball.

Directions: The goalkeeper with the ball starts play with a pass to a teammate. The teams play 5 v 5 and must complete eight consecutive passes before attempting a shot on goal. Play is continuous for 20 minutes. The team scoring the most goals wins.

Variations:

1. Increase the number of players.
2. Restrict passing to two or one touch.

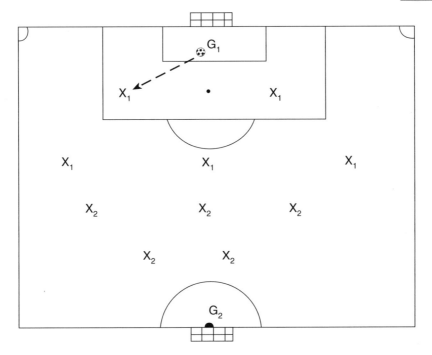

Four Goals

44

Contributor: Gus Constantine, New York Institute of Technology

Emphases: Attack, defense, passing

No. of Players: 10

Equipment Needed: 1 ball, 12 cones, 10 practice jerseys

Setup: Two teams of five players each are positioned within a 40-by-40-yard area bordered by a cone at each corner. Each team wears different-colored practice jerseys. There are four goals. Each goal is one yard wide, marked by two cones, and located at the midpoint of each sideline. The coach, holding a ball, stands in the center of the area.

Directions: The coach starts play by dropping a ball between two opposing players. The team that wins possession of the ball is on attack. The other team is on defense and attempts to go on attack by intercepting the ball. The object of the game is to score by passing the ball to a teammate through any of the four goals. Play continues until one team scores 10 goals.

Variations:

1. Increase or decrease the number of players.

2. Vary the size of the field depending on the number of players, the skill level of the players, or the tactic the coach wishes to emphasize (e.g., to emphasize passing in close space, the field would be smaller).

3. The field can be rectangular of varying sizes. Goals at the long ends count two points and goals on the sides count one point.

4. Players may make attempts on goal only after they make a set number of passes.

5. Increase passing difficulty by requiring two- or one-touch passing.

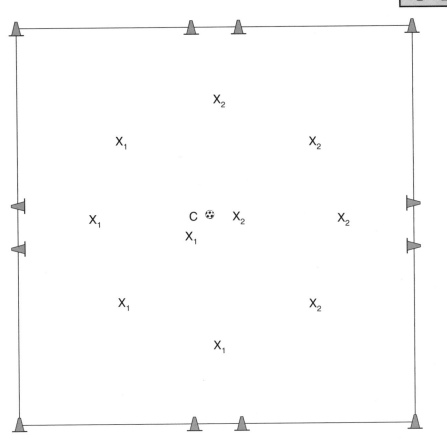

45 Four Versus Four Plus Two Possession

Contributor: Betsy Duerksen, University of Montana

Emphasis: Possession

No. of Players: 10

Equipment Needed: 1 ball, 8 cones, 10 practice jerseys

Setup: The game is played between the penalty area and midfield, using the 18-yard line and midfield line as end lines. Four cones are at equal intervals along each sideline. Two teams, X1 and X2, of four players each, wearing different-colored practice jerseys, are positioned within the playing area. Two other players, N, wearing different-colored practice jerseys from the two teams, are also located within the playing area. One of the X1 players has a ball.

Directions: On a signal from the coach, the four X1s and the two Ns play 6 v 4 keep-away from the X2s, who try to gain possession of the ball. The object of the game is for the six players to keep possession as long as possible. The Ns always play with the team in possession of the ball. One point is scored for each set of five consecutive passes. Play is continuous for 20 minutes. The team with the most points wins.

Variations:

1. Size of playing area can be larger or smaller.
2. Passing can be limited to two or one touch.
3. A point can be scored for stopping a ball on an end line.

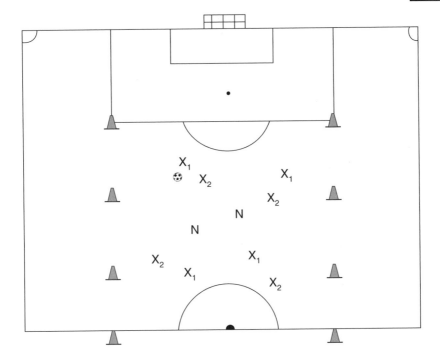

Four Versus Four Two-Minute Game

Contributor: Susan Viscomi, SUNY at Oswego

Emphases: Attack, defense, fitness

No. of Players: 18

Equipment Needed: 5 balls, 8 cones, 2 goals, 16 practice jerseys

Setup: The game is played in an area 44 yards wide by 40 yards long. A cone is at each corner of the area. The width of the penalty area and cones mark the sidelines. A goal is at the midpoint of each end line. There are four teams of four players each. Each team wears different-colored practice jerseys. Two of the teams are positioned opposite each other in each half of the area. The players on the other two teams spread out along each sideline. A goalkeeper is in each goal. One of the goalkeepers holds a ball, and two extra balls are in each goal.

Directions: The goalkeeper with the ball starts a 4 v 4 game by passing to a player on one of the teams in the playing area. The object of the game is both to score and to preserve the lead by not giving up a goal once a team has scored. The goalkeepers and sideline players help keep play continuous by getting the ball back in play after each shot, goal, or out-of-bounds play. The game is over either after two minutes or when one team is ahead 2-0. A team is awarded one point by winning a 1-0 or 2-0 game, or in a 1-1 game by being the team to come from behind to tie. No points are awarded for a 0-0 game. Each team plays each other team once. The team with the most points at the end of round-robin play wins. Tie-breaking rules can be established if two or more teams have the same number of points.

Variation: To promote fitness, increase the time limit of each game to five minutes.

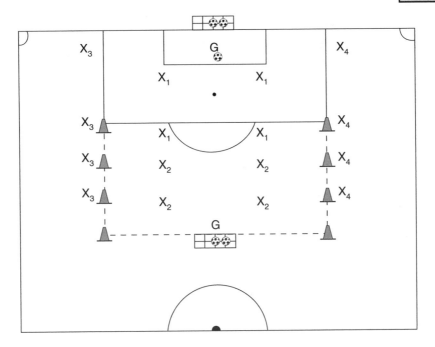

Contributor: Steve Locker, Harvard University

Emphases: Attack, defense

No. of Players: 8

Equipment Needed: 1 ball, 10 cones, 8 practice jerseys

Setup: The game is played in an area 20 yards wide by 30 yards long. A cone is at each corner of the area and on each sideline at midfield. Two goals, four yards wide, are marked by cones and located at the midpoint of each end line. There are two teams of four players each, wearing different-colored practice jerseys. One team is designated as the attacking team and is located within the playing area. One of the attackers has a ball at midfield. The defending team has two players within the playing area and one player in each goal. The players in the goal must stay on their line and may not use their hands.

Directions: The attackers attempt to score in either goal against the two defenders. Each time a team scores, it earns one point and must get the ball back to midfield before beginning another attack on goal. If the defenders intercept the ball, or an attacker plays the ball out-of-bounds, the attackers and defenders switch roles. The new attacking team must get the ball to midfield before attacking either goal. The team scoring the most goals wins.

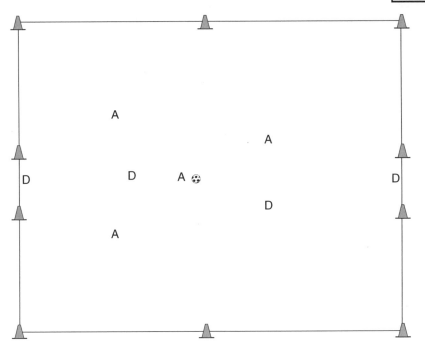

Contributor: Michael A. Costa, Jackson Memorial High School

Emphasis: Defense

No. of Players: 14

Equipment Needed: 1 ball, 4 cones, 2 goals

Setup: The game is played in an area from the 18-yard line to midfield bordered by a cone at each corner. A goal is at the midpoint of the 18-yard line and midfield. A goalkeeper is in each goal. Two teams of six players each, X1 and X2, line up on the end line outside opposite goalposts of the same goal. A player on the X1 team has a ball.

Directions: On a signal from the coach, the X1s begin an attack on the opposite goal. The X2s sprint to get goalside as soon as possible, with the nearest defender moving to shut down the ball and slow the attack. The attacking team must make three passes before it can shoot. Play ends with a shot on goal or loss of ball possession. Both teams then line up facing the opposite direction, and the X2s now attack the opposite goal. The team giving up the fewest number of goals wins.

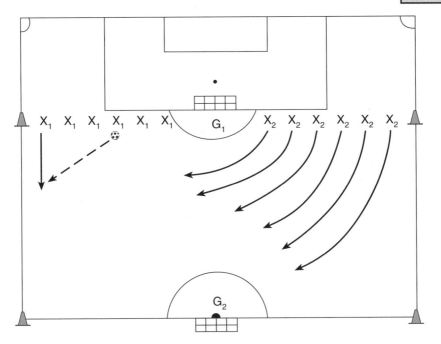

Goals War

Contributor: Tom Breznitsky, Scotch Plains Fanwood High School

Emphases: Attack, defense, goalkeeping

No. of Players: 18

Equipment Needed: 6 balls, 4 cones, 2 goals, 16 practice jerseys

Setup: The game is played in an area the width of the field and 25 yards in each direction from midfield. A cone marks each corner of the area. Two goals are placed back to back in the center circle at midfield. There are two teams, a red team and a blue team, of nine players each. Each team consists of four attackers, four defenders, and one goalkeeper. Four blue attackers face four red defenders and the red goalkeeper in one area, and four red attackers face four blue defenders and the blue goalkeeper in the other area. The blue goalkeeper has a ball. Five extra balls are between the goals.

Directions: The game is started by the blue goalkeeper distributing the ball to a blue attacker in the opposite side of midfield. The blue attackers attempt to score on the red goal. If a goal is scored, the red goalkeeper restarts play by passing to a red attacker in the opposite side of midfield. If a defender intercepts the ball, the ball is passed to that team's attackers in the opposite side of midfield. Play is continuous for several minutes, after which the attackers and defenders on each team switch roles. The team scoring a set number of goals first is the winner.

Variations:

1. Limit the number of touches.
2. Score goals only by heading.
3. Play with two balls at the same time.
4. Increase the numbers of defenders or attackers.

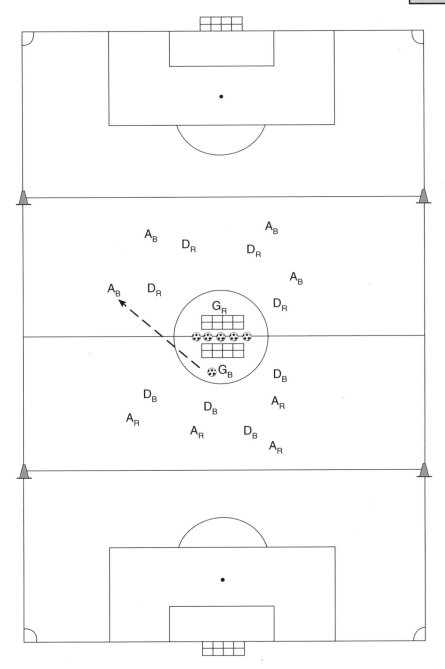

Graham's Quackers

Contributor: Nelson Graham, Wayne Soccer Club

Emphases: Defense, transition play, communication

No. of Players: 8

Equipment Needed: 1 ball, 4 cones, 8 practice jerseys

Setup: Two teams of four players each, wearing different-colored practice jerseys, are positioned within a 20-by-20-yard grid bordered by a cone at each corner. A player on one team has a ball.

Directions: The teams play a 4 v 4 game within the grid. The object of the game is for the team in possession of the ball to score by dribbling the ball over the opponent's end line. After a score, play is restarted by the team scored upon. The defending team tries to shut down the attack and gain possession of the ball to go on attack. The game is played with the following restrictions: 1. When the defenders win the ball, the player with the ball must count to "5 one thousand" before dribbling forward or passing to a teammate. The teammates can move immediately anywhere in the grid. 2. The team that lost possession must run back to their end line, touch it, and come back quickly on defense. The first player to touch the end line moves to pressure the player with the ball, communicating to teammates by shouting, "I've got ball." All other defenders support the pressurizing player and communicate to that player that support is there. Play continues in this fashion for a predetermined time or until a set number of scores are made.

Variations:

1. Decrease or increase the grid size and number of players.
2. Add goals.
3. Have attackers maintain possession after scoring.
4. Have defenders run backward to end line before touching it.

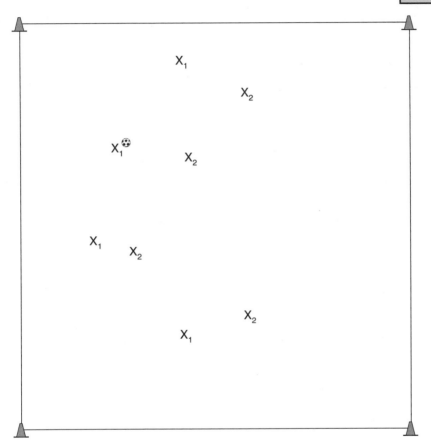

Half Court

Contributor: Tim Wheaton, Harvard University

Emphases: Attack, defense

No. of Players: 13

Equipment Needed: 1 ball, 1 goal, 8 practice jerseys

Setup: There are three teams of four players each, X1, X2, and X3, wearing different-colored practice jerseys. The X1s and X2s spread out in the penalty area. An X1 has a ball. The X3s stand around the penalty area. A goal is at the midpoint of the end line. A goalkeeper is in goal.

Directions: The X1 with the ball starts a 4 v 4 game. In the initial possession, the X1s may shoot on goal at any time. On any loss of possession the team gaining possession must dribble or pass the ball to a sideline or the 18-yard line before attacking the goal. Balls going out-of-bounds are put back into play with a throw-in by a player on the team not causing the out-of-bounds ball. A goal save is put back into play by the goalkeeper passing the ball to a player on the opposite team. Each time a goal is scored, the team not scoring is replaced by the team outside the penalty area. The team scoring the most goals in a set time wins.

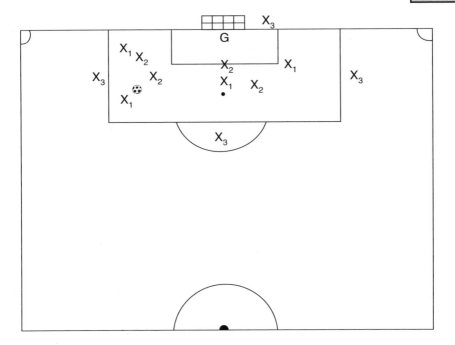

Head It, Catch It

Contributor: Rob Chesney, Montclair State University

Emphases: Communication, fitness

No. of Players: 7 to 15

Equipment Needed: 1 or 2 balls, cones

Setup: The game is played in the midfield circle or a similar-sized circle formed by cones. Ten players stand at equally spaced intervals around the perimeter of the circle. The players face the coach who is in the middle of the circle with a ball.

Directions: On the coach's signal, all the players begin to jog clockwise around the circle keeping their original spacing. After two warm-up laps, the coach, with a ball in hand, approaches one of the players, throws the ball to the player, and calls out either "Head it" or "Catch it." The player must get the ball back to the coach using the action opposite to the coach's command (e.g., if the coach says "Head it" the player catches the ball and tosses it back to the coach). The coach can then move to another player or continue with the same player. A player making a mistake steps out of the path of the other players and does 10 push-ups before returning to the original space around the circle. The players continue jogging at all times. Play continues for 10 to 20 minutes.

Variations:

1. Add another coach with a ball, both coaches working at the same time with the players.

2. Increase the pace.

3. Add additional commands (e.g., kneel or jump). In response to the command, the player does the opposite action.

4. A player is eliminated when a mistake is made until only one player is left.

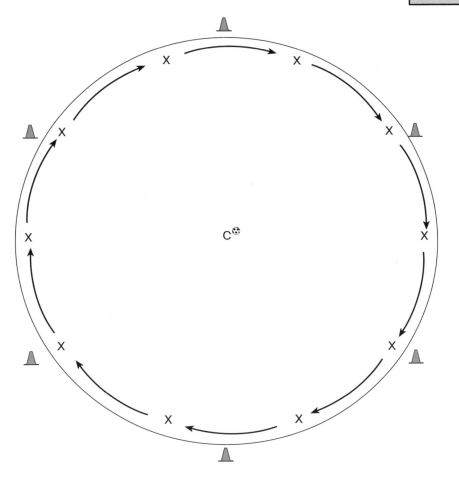

53 Hellgate

Contributor: Candy Canzoneri, Otterbein College

Emphases: Possession, movement off the ball, fitness

No. of Players: 10

Equipment Needed: 1 ball, 5 cones, 5 practice jerseys, 1 stopwatch

Setup: Two teams of five players each are positioned within a 40-yard square grid. One team wears practice jerseys. A cone is at each corner of the grid. A gate is formed by placing a cone five yards from one of the corner cones. A coach with a stopwatch stands outside the grid.

Directions: The coach designates one team to start with possession of the ball. The other team is on defense and attempts to intercept the ball. If the team with ball possession completes 10 consecutive passes, each player on defense must sprint out the marked gate, sprint one circuit around the grid, and reenter the grid through the gate. The coach begins timing as soon as the 10th pass is completed. After 40 seconds the team with ball possession may begin passing again, regardless of how many defenders are back in the grid. Play is continuous for a predetermined time.

Variations:

1. Change the size of the grid or number of players.
2. Increase passing difficulty by requiring one- or two-touch passing.

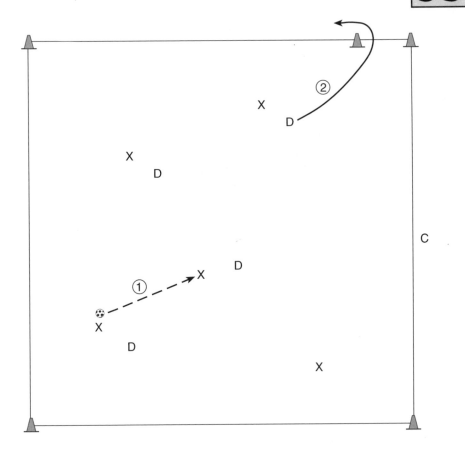

Hot Box

Contributor: Kevin McCarthy, Columbia University

Emphases: Attack, defense

No. of Players: 14

Equipment Needed: 8 balls, 6 cones, 2 goals

Setup: The game is played in an area 30 yards wide by 20 yards long. Cones are used to mark the corners and midfield of the area. A goal is at the midpoint of each end line. A supply of balls is in each goal. Two teams of six players each are within the area. Three players from each team, designated as either attackers or defenders, are within their respective attacking and defending halves of the area. A goalkeeper is in each goal. One of the goalkeepers has a ball.

Directions: The goalkeeper with the ball starts a 6 v 6 game with a pass to a teammate. The teams play 3 v 3 within each half of the area. Players may pass the ball across midfield to a teammate, but may not move into the opposite area. Attackers may take shots on goal at any time, but defenders may take only one-touch shots on goal from a pass back across midfield. Play is continuous for 20 minutes. The team scoring the most goals wins.

Variations:

1. Eliminate the midfield line and the restrictions on players moving anywhere in the area.

2. Permit one or more defenders to move into the attacking zone creating a numerical attacking advantage.

3. Play with a one- or two-touch limit.

Hot Box

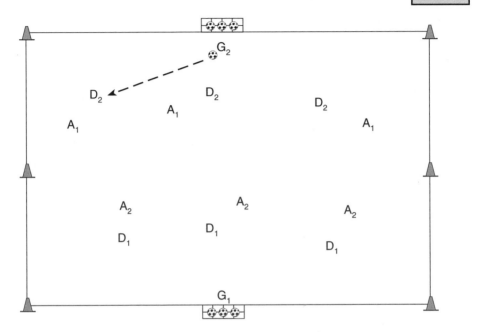

Contributor: Matthew Smith, Johns Hopkins University

Emphases: Transition play, communication

No. of Players: 8

Equipment Needed: 3 balls, 4 cones, 1 goal, 6 practice jerseys

Setup: Two teams of three players each, wearing different-colored practice jerseys, are positioned within an area 20 yards wide by 30 yards long. A cone marks each of the area's corners. A goal is at the midpoint of one end line. A goalkeeper is in the goal. A neutral player, with three balls, stands on the end line opposite the goalkeeper.

Directions: The neutral player starts play by passing a ball to space. The team gaining possession is on attack and attempts to score against the other team. If the defensive team intercepts the ball, it is played out to the neutral player. The defensive team then goes on attack and moves to receive a pass from the neutral player. If the attacking team scores, it stays on attack and restarts play by moving to receive a pass from the neutral player. Play is restarted after a ball goes out-of-bounds by a pass in from a player on the team that did not cause the ball to go out.

Variation: The neutral player can be an active part of the attacking team.

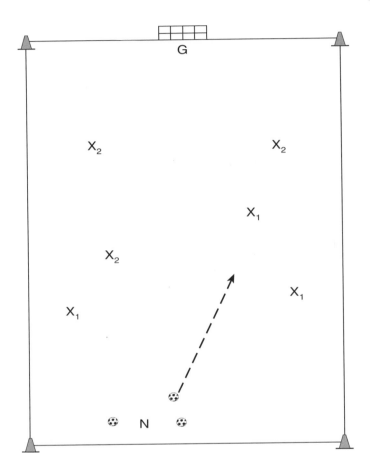

Marking Game

Contributor: Michael Coven, Brandeis University

Emphasis: Defense

No. of Players: 12

Equipment Needed: 1 ball, 2 goals, 10 practice jerseys

Setup: Two teams of five players each, wearing different-colored practice jerseys, are located within one-half of a soccer field. A goal is at the midpoint of the end line and midfield line. A goalkeeper is in each goal. One goalkeeper has a ball.

Directions: The goalkeeper with the ball starts play with a pass to a teammate. The teams play 5 v 5, but each player may only defend the same opponent throughout the game. No player can cover for a teammate if that player gets beat by an opponent. The player who was beat must recover and get goalside of the opponent. Play is continuous for 20 minutes. The team scoring the most goals wins.

Variations:

1. Increase the number of players.
2. Restrict passing to two or one touch.

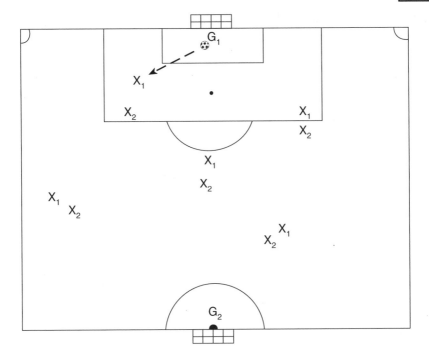

Contributor: Dan Kilday, New Jersey Institute of Technology

Emphases: Attack, defense, transition play

No. of Players: 16

Equipment Needed: 1 ball, 24 disc cones, 2 goals, 12 practice jerseys

Setup: As shown in the diagram, a regulation soccer field is divided by disc cones into defensive, middle, and attacking thirds lengthwise, and into right, central, and left lanes along the width. The attacking and defending thirds will be determined by the direction of the attacking teams. There are two teams of seven players each. Each team is comprised of six field players and a goalkeeper. Each team's field players wear different-colored practice jerseys. Two players from each team are located in each third of the field. There are two flank players, one in the right lane and one in the left lane. The field players may not move out of the central zone and their third of the field. The flank players, who play with the team in possession of the ball, may move the length of the field within their respective lanes. A goalkeeper from each team is in the appropriate goal. One of the goalkeepers has a ball.

Directions: The goalkeeper with the ball starts the game with a pass to a teammate in that team's defensive third. The object of the game is to advance the ball into each third of the field, using the flank players, and finish with a shot on goal. Following a goal or save, the goalkeeper who made the save or was scored on restarts play in the opposite direction. A defensive team intercepting the ball in any third must pass the ball to a flank player before attacking the goal. Play continues until a set number of goals are scored.

Variation: One player may advance into the next third after a pass is made into that third. This will create a numerical advantage for the attackers in each third.

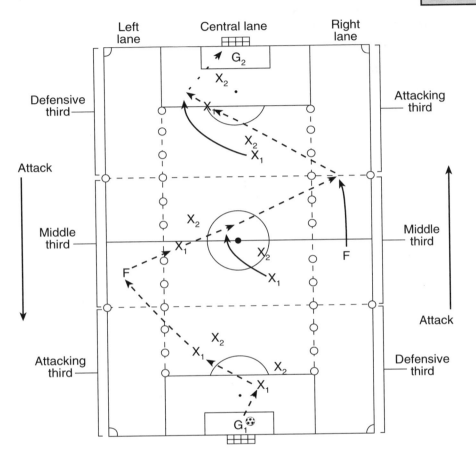

One on One

Contributors: Editors

Emphases: Attack, defense, goalkeeping

No. of Players: 13

Equipment Needed: 6 balls, 1 goal

Setup: The game is played in one-half of a soccer field. There are two teams of six players each. One team starts as the defending team and lines up behind the end line near a goalpost. Each player has a ball. The other team is the attacking team and lines up at midfield near the center circle. A goalkeeper is in goal.

Directions: Each defender in turn will kick a goal kick toward the center circle. The waiting attacker receives the ball, dribbles toward the goal, and attempts to shoot on goal. The defender who made the goal kick runs to tackle the attacker. If the defender is successful, the play ends, and the players go to the end of their respective lines. If the attacker is able to maintain possession to the edge of the penalty area, the defender releases, and the goalkeeper plays the attacker 1 v 1. The attackers score five points for each goal, and the defenders score one point each time an attacker fails to score. The team ahead after a set time or number of goals is the winner.

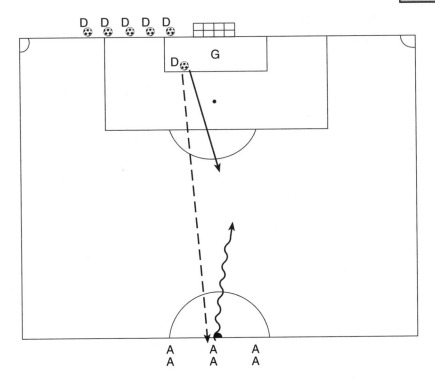

59

Ostende Split

Contributor: Rob Searl, St. John Fisher College

Emphases: Attack, defense

No. of Players: 13

Equipment Needed: 1 ball, 4 cones, 2 goals, 12 practice jerseys

Setup: The game is played in one-half of a soccer field with a goal at the midpoint of the end line. Two cones, six feet apart, mark a small goal on each side of the field at midfield. Two teams of six players each wear different-colored practice jerseys. One team has been designated as on attack and the other team on defense. The teams are located within the playing area. One attacker has a ball in the midfield center area. A goalkeeper is in goal.

Directions: The attacker with the ball starts play with a pass to a teammate. The attackers attempt to score on goal. The defenders attempt to gain possession of the ball and clear or pass the ball out through one of the small goals at midfield. When a defending team scores through a small goal, it becomes the attacking team, and the former attacking team goes on defense. One point is awarded only when an attacking team scores on the regulation goal. The team with the most points after a predetermined time is the winner.

Variations:

1. To go on attack, a defending team player must dribble the ball through one of the small goals.

2. To go on attack, a defending team player must pass the ball through one of the small goals to a teammate.

3. Limit touches for the attackers.

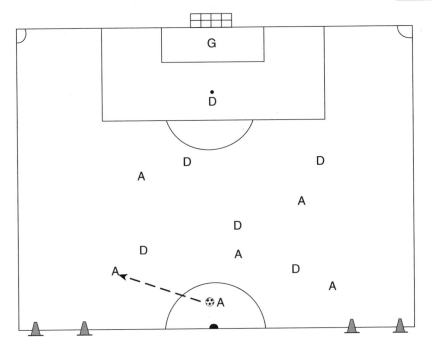

60

Phenomenal Finishing

Contributor: Tracey Ranieri, SUNY at Oneonta

Emphases: Attack, defense, fitness

No. of Players: 18

Equipment Needed: 6 balls, 4 cones, 2 goals, 16 practice jerseys

Setup: A playing area of 50-by-50 yards is marked by a cone at each corner. A goal is at the midpoint of opposite end lines. Four teams of four players each wear different-colored practice jerseys. Two teams, X1 and X2, are positioned within the area. One other team is behind each goal. A player on the X1 team has a ball. A goalkeeper is in each goal. Extra balls are in each goal.

Directions: Team X1 starts play by attacking and attempting to score against X2's defense. Should the X1s score or play the ball beyond X2's end line, the X3s immediately get possession of a ball from the goalkeeper and attack the X1s. The X2s now rest behind the goal they defended. If the X3s score or play the ball beyond X1's end line, the X4s immediately attack the X3s. The X1s rest behind the goal they defended. If a defending team intercepts the ball, or the goalkeeper saves a shot on goal, the same teams continue play until a goal is scored or the ball is played over the end line. Regulation rules are followed for balls played over the sidelines. Play continues for a predetermined time or until a set number of goals are scored by one team.

Variations:

1. Increase or decrease the number of players or size of playing area.

2. Limit play to two or one touch.

3. Require specific combination plays before shooting on goal.

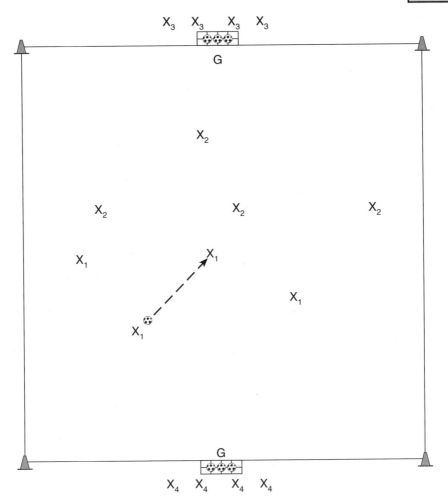

Possession Game

Contributor: Fran O'Leary, Dartmouth College

Emphases: Possession, passing

No. of Players: 16

Equipment Needed: 1 ball, 4 cones, 16 practice jerseys

Setup: The game is played in a 30-by-30-yard grid bordered by a cone at each corner. There are two teams of eight players each, wearing different-colored practice jerseys. Four players from each team are located within the grid. The other four players on each team are wall players, with one player from each team positioned along each sideline. One field player has a ball.

Directions: On a signal from the coach, the team in possession of the ball plays keep-away from the other team who attempts to gain possession. The object of the game is to complete as many consecutive passes as possible. One point is scored for each 10 consecutive passes. The field players may use the players on their team who are along the sideline. Wall passes are limited to one-touch passes. The wall players cannot pass the ball back to the player who passed the ball to the wall player. Wall players cannot enter the grid or interfere with any field player. Loss of ball possession results from any violation. Play is continuous for 12 minutes with the field and wall players changing positions every 2 or 3 minutes. The team with the most points at the end of time is the winner.

Variations:

1. To make the game more difficult, decrease the size of the grid or limit the field players to one-touch passing.

2. To make the game less difficult, increase the size of the grid or allow the wall players a second touch.

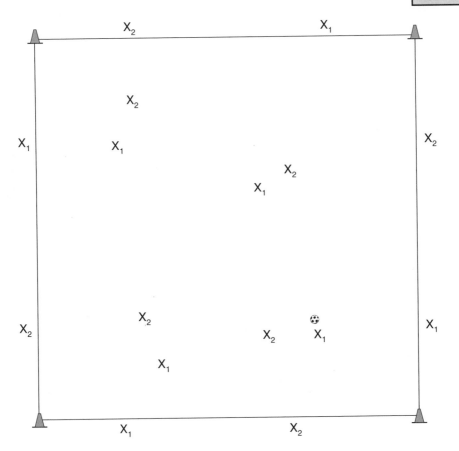

Press Five

Contributor: Stephen J. Swanson, Stanford University

Emphasis: Transition play

No. of Players: 12

Equipment Needed: 1 ball, 30 cones, 10 practice jerseys

Setup: The game is played in an area that is half-field in length and the width of the penalty area. Ten cones are used to mark each sideline. Arcs, with a radius of five yards marked by five cones, are located at the midpoint of the end line and half-field line. A goalkeeper is in each arc. One goalkeeper has a ball. There are two teams of five players each, wearing different-colored practice jerseys. The field players may play anywhere in the area but may not enter the arcs.

Directions: The goalkeeper with the ball starts play with a free pass to a player on the team facing the opposite goalkeeper. The object of the game is for the team in possession of the ball to pass it in the air to the opposite goalkeeper while the team without the ball defends. If the defensive team gains possession of the ball, they quickly try to pass the ball to the goalkeeper facing them. A point is scored each time the ball is passed in the air to the goalkeeper. Once the goal is scored, the goalkeeper immediately restarts play with a free pass to a player on the team that did not score. Play is continuous for 20 minutes. The team with the most points wins. The coach emphasizes immediate transition play, pointing out that attackers moving quickly and making early passes can exploit the other team in slow transition.

Variations:

1. For advanced players, place the goalkeepers on benches. This way the passes must be more accurate as the goalkeepers must catch the ball while on the bench for a goal to be scored.

2. Add one or two neutral players, who always play with the team on attack.

3. Limit touches or require one-touch passes to the goalkeepers.

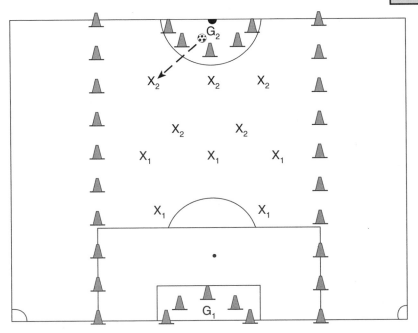

4. To make the game easier, enlarge size of arc or allow passes on the ground to the goalkeepers to count as goals.

5. Use three teams to provide rest for one team and permit time for coach to discuss the resting team's play with them.

63 Pressing Game

Contributor: Fran O'Leary, Dartmouth College

Emphases: Defense, possession

No. of Players: 12

Equipment Needed: 6 balls, 4 cones, 2 goals, 10 practice jerseys

Setup: The game is played in an area 50 yards long by 44 yards wide bordered by a cone at each corner. A goal is at the midpoint of each end line. Two teams of five players each, wearing different-colored practice jerseys, are located within the playing area. A goalkeeper is in each goal. One of the goalkeepers holds a ball. Extra balls are in each goal.

Directions: A 5 v 5 game starts with a pass from the goalkeeper with the ball to a teammate. Regulation soccer rules are followed until one team scores. The goalkeeper on the team scored upon restarts play with a pass to a teammate. When a team scores, it can play only possession ball and cannot score again until the opposing team has scored. When the team behind scores, the game returns to normal 5 v 5 play with both teams attempting to score. The team that is one goal ahead at the end of a predetermined time is the winner. Should the score be tied at this time, play can either continue until a goal is scored or teams can take penalty kicks to determine a winner.

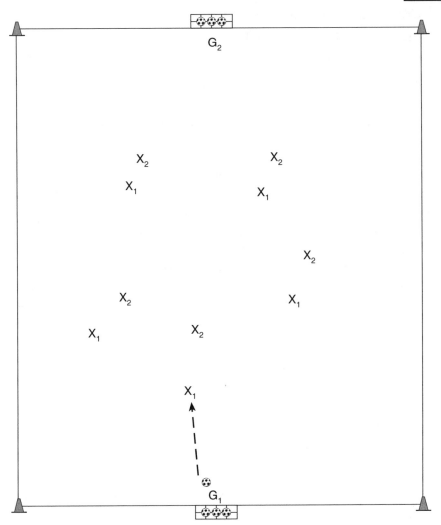

Pressure the Ball 1-2-3

Contributor: Susan Viscomi, SUNY at Oswego

Emphases: Defense, attack

No. of Players: 6

Equipment Needed: 3 balls, 8 cones

Setup: The game is played in a grid 30 yards long by 10 yards wide. Cones at each corner and at 10-yard intervals along each sideline divide the larger grid into three 10-by-10-yard grids. Three attackers are in a single file outside one end line. Three defenders, each with a ball, are in a single file outside the opposite end line.

Directions: The game starts with a serve from the first defender to the first attacker. The defender follows the pass with a sprint to pressure the player with the ball. The object of the game is for the defender to gain possession of the ball or force the attacker to play the ball out-of-bounds, while the attacker attempts to beat the defender and dribble the ball over the defender's end line. A *quick start, slow arrival* defensive approach is emphasized to ensure the defender is balanced to play good defense. Patience is stressed so that the defender learns the best time to attempt to win the ball. A defender scores points in relation to the grid where the ball is won or forced out-of-bounds: three points in the grid nearest the attacker's end line, two points in the middle grid, and one point in the grid nearest the defender's end line. The attacker earns one point for dribbling the ball over the defender's end line. Play stops after the defender gains possession or forces the ball out-of-bounds or when the attacker dribbles the ball over the defender's end line, and the next ball is served. After all three balls have been played, the players change roles. The group of three players with the most points after a predetermined number of rounds is the winner.

Variations:

1. Vary the types of serves from defender to attacker.
2. Vary the grid size.

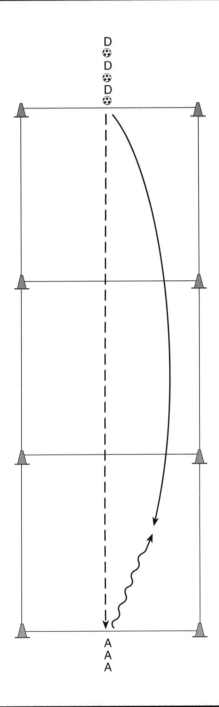

Quick Counter Game

Contributor: Helio D'Anna, Union College

Emphases: Attack, defense, transition play

No. of Players: 6

Equipment Needed: 1 ball, 4 cones, 2 goals

Setup: The game is played in a 40-by-40-yard area bordered by a cone at each corner. Two mini-goals are at the midpoint of opposite ends of the area. There are two teams of three players each. One team has been designated as attackers and the other team is on defense. The attackers stand on one end line, 10 yards apart from each other, facing the opposite end line. The defenders are facing the attackers. Each defender is directly opposite and five yards from each attacker. A coach with a ball stands behind the defenders.

Directions: The coach starts play by passing to any attacker. The three attackers move immediately to attack the opposite goal. The defender directly opposite the attacker who received the pass must run and touch the end line five yards away before playing defense. The other two defenders play containment defense as soon as the pass is made and must wait for the third defender to get back to begin aggressive defense. The attackers try to complete an attack on goal before the third defender gets back. After a shot is taken, the players reverse roles and the game starts again in the opposite direction. The first team to score a set number of goals wins.

Variations:

1. Use regulation goals with a goalkeeper in each goal.
2. Allow the team that scores to stay on attack.
3. Increase the number of players.

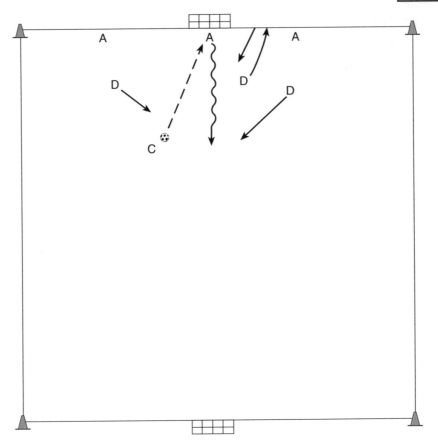

Quick Play

> **Contributor:** Jim Felix, Buckingham, Browne, and Nichols School
>
> **Emphases:** Attack, defense
>
> **No. of Players:** 18
>
> **Equipment Needed:** 1 ball, 12 disc cones, 8 upright cones, 2 goals, 16 practice jerseys

Setup: The game is played within a soccer field using the regulation sidelines and the penalty area lines extended to the sidelines as end lines. The field is divided into two end areas of 18 yards each and a 40-yard midfield. Upright cones are placed along the sidelines and disc cones across the field to mark the three areas. A goal is at the midpoint of each end line. There are two teams of nine players each, X1 and X2. Each team consists of eight field players and one goalkeeper. Each team's field players wear different-colored practice jerseys. The field players are located within the midfield area. A goalkeeper is in each goal. One of the X1s has a ball.

Directions: The X1 player with the ball starts play with a pass to a teammate. The X1s move immediately on attack and the X2s attempt to gain possession and go on attack. Regulation rules are followed except for the restriction of one touch in the end areas and two touches in the midfield area. Play is continuous for 30 minutes. The team scoring the most goals wins.

Variations:

1. Increase the number of players.
2. Vary the number of touches allowed.
3. Vary the size of the areas.

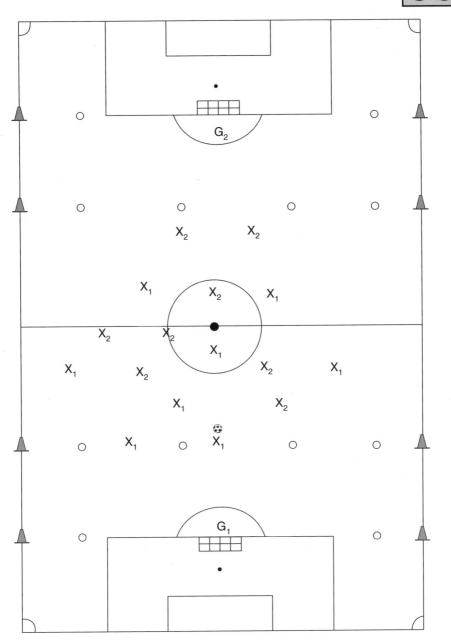

Contributor: Fred Schmalz, University of Evansville

Emphases: Possession, fitness

No. of Players: 21

Equipment Needed: 12 cones, 6 practice jerseys, 12 balls

Setup: Three 12-by-12-yard grids are located in one-half of the field. One grid is in the center circle and two grids are at the end line corners. Three groups of seven players each are in each grid. Two of the players in each group have been designated to start as defenders in the middle of each grid. These players wear practice jerseys. The other five players in each group, one with a ball, spread around the grid perimeter. To maintain game intensity when a ball goes out of a grid, extra balls are located by each grid.

Directions: The three groups play 5 v 2 keep-away games. For best effect, restrict games to two touch. On a signal from the coach, the five players on the outside of each grid sprint clockwise to the next grid. While these players are sprinting, the two middle players remaining in each grid one-touch pass to each other until all the next five players arrive in the grid. The last two players of each group arriving in the next grid become the middle players, and the keep-away games continue. Play is continuous for a predetermined time.

Variations:

1. Use fewer players and play 4 v 2 or 3 v 1 in each grid.
2. Play one-touch games.
3. On the signal by the coach for the players to sprint, the ball is kicked to the next grid before the players sprint.
4. Grids can be smaller but no less than 10-by-10 yards.

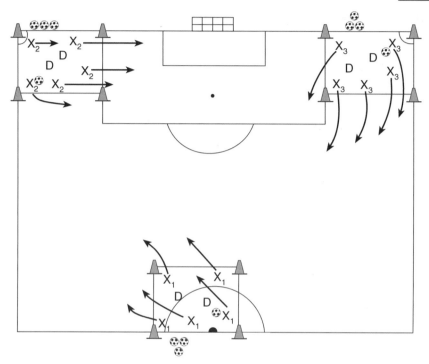

Shoot and Defend

Contributor: Brian Dooley, Barry University

Emphases: Transition play, defense, shooting

No. of Players: 14

Equipment Needed: 6 balls, 4 cones, 2 goals, 12 practice jerseys

Setup: The game is played in a grid 40 yards long by 30 yards wide bordered by a cone at each corner. A goal is at the midpoint of each end line. A goalkeeper, with three balls, is in each goal. There are two teams of six players each, X1 and X2, wearing different-colored practice jerseys. Three players from each team are within the grid, and the other three players are behind their goal.

Directions: One goalkeeper starts the game with a pass to a teammate. The teams on the field play 3 v 3 until a shot on goal is taken. The team that allows a shot to be taken is replaced by the resting three players, who must immediately attack the other team. If a defending team gains possession of the ball, they immediately counterattack. The only way a team is replaced is by giving up a shot on goal. Play is continuous for 20 minutes. The team with the most goals wins.

Variations:

1. Teams change only when a goalkeeper makes a save on goal.
2. Teams change only when a goal is scored.

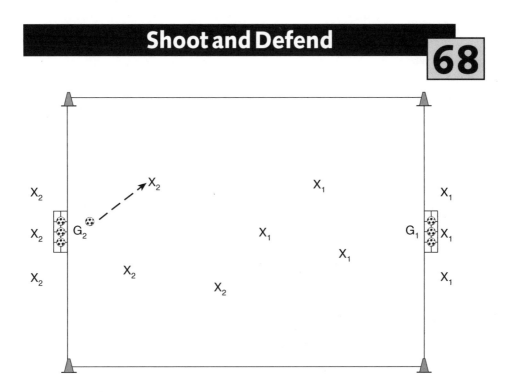

Small-Sided Finishing Game

Contributor: Michael Mooney, SUNY at Geneseo

Emphases: Attack, defense, shooting, goalkeeping

No. of Players: 14

Equipment Needed: 10 balls, 4 cones, 2 goals, 1 stopwatch

Setup: The game is played in an area 25 yards wide by 30 yards long bordered by a cone at each corner. A goal is on the midpoint of each end line. There are two teams of seven players each, divided into three pairs and a goalkeeper. Each team has one pair of players within the area. The other two pairs from each team spread along the sidelines. A goalkeeper is in each goal. The field players may go anywhere within the field. The players on the sideline may only move along that line. Extra balls are next to each goal. One of the goalkeepers holds a ball.

Directions: The goalkeeper with the ball starts play with a pass to a teammate. The pair in possession of the ball attempts to shoot on the opponent's goal while the other pair attempts to gain possession and move on attack. The object of the game is for each attacking team to get off as many shots on goal as possible in two minutes. Every two minutes, the coach signals time, and a pair from each team on the sideline change positions with the field players. The team with the ball when time was called keeps possession. The goalkeepers may distribute the ball only to their teammates. Sideline players may be used only for wall passes. If a ball goes over the end line, including a score, the goalkeeper in that goal immediately distributes a ball to a teammate. If a ball goes over a sideline, the goalkeeper on the team last in possession of the ball immediately distributes a ball to a teammate. Play is continuous for a predetermined time or until a set number of goals are scored.

Variations:

1. Shorten or lengthen time periods.
2. Increase the number of field players.
3. Restrict passes to two or one touch.

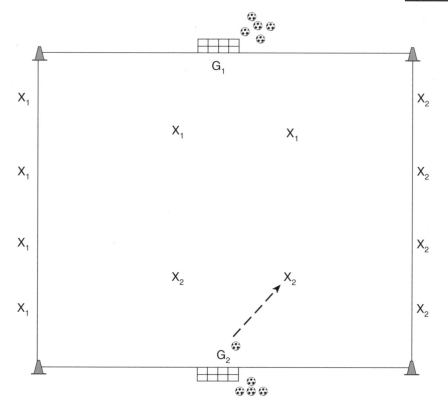

Support Game

Contributor: Denis Mayer, Piscataway High School

Emphases: Movement off the ball, possession, defense

No. of Players: 6

Equipment Needed: 6 balls, 8 cones, 6 practice jerseys

Setup: The game is played in a 30-by-30-yard grid bordered by a cone at each corner. Two goals, each 12 feet wide and marked by two cones, are at the midpoint of opposite end lines. Two teams of three players each, wearing different-colored practice jerseys, are within the grid. A coach, with six balls, stands just outside the grid.

Directions: A 3 v 3 game is started by the coach tossing or punting a ball up for grabs. The player who controls the ball looks to pass to teammates who are moving into supporting positions. The team in possession must complete five consecutive passes before shooting. The defenders attempt to gain possession and begin their passing. Once a team has completed five passes, it is *on* and may shoot until it scores a goal or the opponents intercept the ball and complete five consecutive passes. If the on team regains possession before the opponents complete the five passes, it may shoot on goal immediately. Passes are counted aloud. When a team is on, this should be clearly announced. At this point, it is necessary to count only for the team attempting to be on. Play is continuous until one team scores a set number of goals.

Variations:

1. Vary the number of passes needed to be on.

2. Increase the number of players and the size of the playing area (e.g., play a 10 v 10 game in a half field using goals and goalkeepers).

3. Restrict passes to two and one touch.

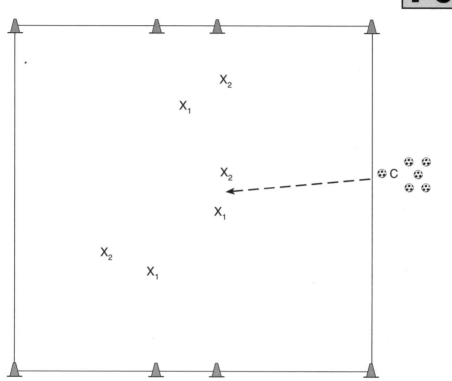

Switch and Finish

Contributor: Andrew Crawford, Hilbert College

Emphases: Attack, defense

No. of Players: 16

Equipment Needed: 8 balls, 16 cones, 8 practice jerseys

Setup: The game is played in a full field. There are two teams of four players each, wearing different-colored practice jerseys. Each team consists of two attackers and two defenders. Each team's attackers and the other team's defenders are positioned within opposite penalty areas. Six neutral players, two central midfielders (CMs), and four outside midfielders (OMs), support both teams. The two CMs are positioned in the center of the field. Each OM must stay in the area between the sideline and a parallel line of cones 10 to 15 yards inside the sideline. A goalkeeper is in each goal. Four balls are in each goal. One goalkeeper holds a ball.

Directions: The goalkeeper with the ball starts play with an outlet throw to OM1 (1). OM1 plays the ball to CM1 (2) who drops the ball back to CM2 (3). CM2 switches field with a pass to OM3 (4). Following this pass, the CMs move forward to support the attackers (5). OM3 dribbles to the end line (6) and crosses the ball to the penalty area (7) for the attackers and midfielders to shoot on goal against the defenders (8). After a goal, goal save, or missed shot, the goalkeeper restarts play with an outlet throw to OM2 (9). Play continues in this manner for a set time, after which the attackers and defenders switch roles. The CMs play in both directions. The team scoring the most goals after a set time wins.

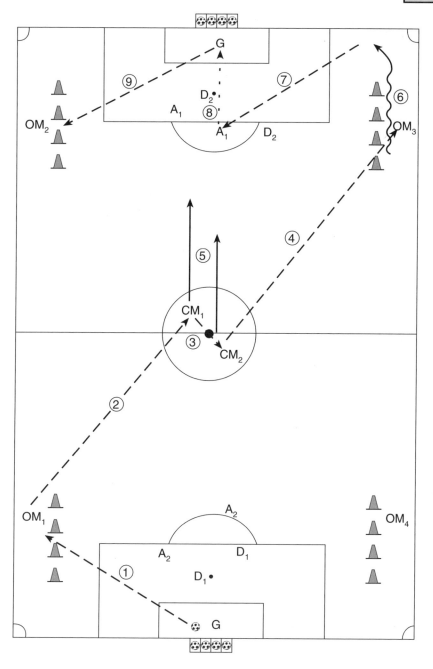

Target Attack

Contributor: Michelle Morgan, Amherst College
Emphases: Attack, possession, passing, shooting
No. of Players: 14
Equipment Needed: 7 balls, 15 disc cones, 2 goals, 12 practice jerseys

Setup: The game is played in one-half of a soccer field using the goal line and midfield line as end lines. The playing area is divided in half by 15 disc cones spread at equal intervals across the middle of the area. A goal is at the midpoint of each end line. Two teams of six players each, X1 and X2, wear different-colored practice jerseys. Four X2s and two X1s are in one-half of the area with two X2s and two X1s in the other half. The remaining two X1s stand by the goal on the end line of the 2 v 2 area. The players are restricted to their half of the playing area. A goalkeeper is in each goal. One goalkeeper has a ball. Three extra balls are in each goal.

Directions: The goalkeeper with the ball starts play with a pass to any of the X2s, who play possession against the X1s until an X2 can make a good penetrating pass to any X2 in the other half of the area. If the pass is successful, the X2s in that area play 2 v 2 with the X1s, with emphases on turning and shooting, taking players on, and support. If a goal is scored or the ball goes over the end line, the X1s on the end line enter the area and two X2s in the other half leave the area. The keeper restarts play with a pass to any of the X1s, who play 4 v 2 until they can make a pass to an X1 in the other half, where 2 v 2 play begins. If the attackers lose possession in the defensive half (the 4 v 2 area), the two new attackers look to shoot immediately. If the attackers lose possession in the attacking half (the 2 v 2 area), the defenders play the ball back to the keeper. Play begins in the opposite direction with both teams making the appropriate transition to offense and defense. A ball going over a sideline is put back in play with a throw-in. Play continues for 20 minutes. The team scoring the most goals wins.

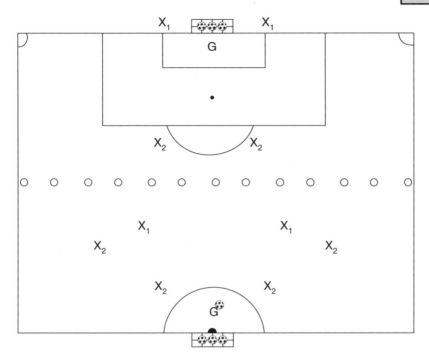

Variations:

1. Allow one player to cross midfield to support the attacking team creating a 3 v 2 situation.

2. Allow two players to cross midfield to support the attacking team creating a 4 v 2 situation.

3. Eliminate the halfway line and remove the movement restriction while maintaining the transition rules.

Team Prep Game

73

Contributor: Gene Chyzowych, Columbia High School

Emphases: Attack, defense

No. of Players: 22

Equipment Needed: 12 balls, 2 goals, 20 practice jerseys

Setup: Two teams of 11 players each are positioned within a soccer field. One team wears red practice jerseys and the other team wears blue practice jerseys. A goalkeeper is in each goal. The red goalkeeper has a ball. Extra balls are behind each goal.

Directions: The starting team plays the reserve team in a full-field scrimmage game. To start the game, the red goalkeeper punts to the blue team. The blue team receives the ball and attacks the red goal. The attacking team gives 100-percent effort. The defending team gives a 75-percent effort and does not attempt to intercept the ball. Play ends with a shot on the red goal, regardless of whether a goal is scored, the goal is missed, or the goalkeeper saves the shot. Play is restarted immediately with a punt by the blue goalkeeper. Both teams move quickly to play the next punt. The game continues in this fashion for 30 minutes. The team scoring the most goals wins.

Variations:

1. Increase defensive effort to 100 percent.
2. Restrict play to two touch, then one touch.

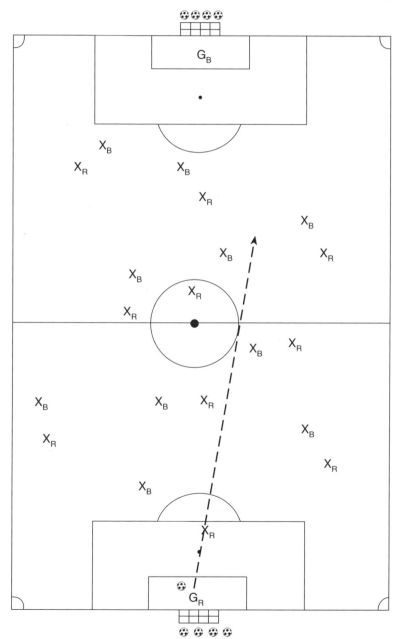

Three Versus Three Plus Three

Contributor: Fred Schmalz, University of Evansville

Emphases: Possession, transition play, passing

No. of Players: 9

Equipment Needed: 1 ball, 4 cones, 9 practice jerseys

Setup: The game is played in an area 40 yards long by 25 yards wide bordered by a cone at each corner. Three groups of three players each, wearing different-colored practice jerseys, are located within the area. One group, X1, has been designated to start in the middle as defenders. The other two groups, X2 and X3, spread around the perimeter of the area. A player on one of these groups has a ball.

Directions: The two perimeter groups play keep-away from the three middle players. Whenever the ball goes out-of-bounds or the middle group gains possession of the ball, the team that last played the ball goes into the middle. When a middle group intercepts the ball, it tries to get the ball to either end line (within one yard of either side of line) before switching places. One point is scored each time a middle group gets the ball to an end line. The coach keeps score and calls out which team goes to the middle. Play continues for a predetermined time. The team with the most points wins.

Variations:

1. Require two- or one-touch play.

2. Have several games going on simultaneously near each other so more players are involved.

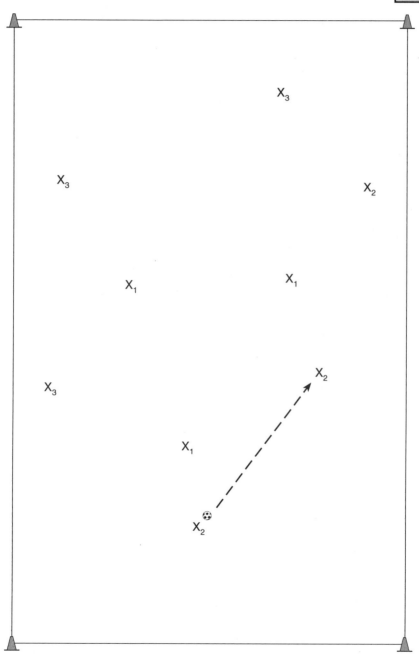

Three Versus Three Plus Two

Contributor: Joseph A. Luxbacher, University of Pittsburgh

Emphases: Attack, defense

No. of Players: 10

Equipment Needed: 1 ball, 4 cones, 2 goals, 6 practice jerseys

Setup: The game is played in an area 35 yards long by 25 yards wide marked by a cone at each corner. Two teams of three players each, wearing different-colored practice jerseys, are positioned within the area. Two other neutral players are also within the area. A goal is at the midpoint of each end line with a goalkeeper in each goal. Each team is assigned a goal to defend. A player on one team has a ball.

Directions: On a signal from the coach, the team with the ball begins play by attempting to score. The opposing team tries to intercept the ball and go on attack. Regulation soccer rules are in effect. The two neutral players play with the team in possession of the ball creating a 5 v 3 advantage for the attackers. Play is continuous for 20 minutes. The team with the most goals wins.

Variation: Limit the attackers to two-touch play.

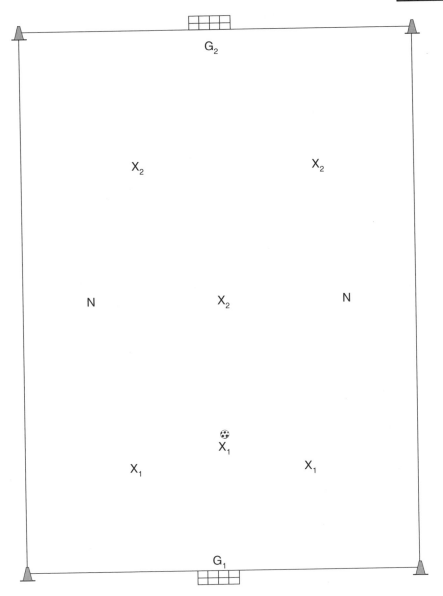

Three Versus Three Transitional

Contributor: Andrew Lowery, Sparta High School

Emphases: Attack, defense, transition play

No. of Players: 18

Equipment Needed: 1 ball, 8 cones, 18 practice jerseys

Setup: The game is played in a grid 30 yards long by 20 yards wide bordered by a cone at each corner. A goal, marked by two cones five yards apart, is at the midpoint of each end line. The players are grouped in teams of three, each team wearing different-colored practice jerseys. Two teams, X1 and X2, are positioned within the grid. A player on the X1 team has a ball. The remaining teams are located equally behind each goal.

Directions: The X1s start the game by moving to attack the goal defended by the X2s. If the X1s score or the X2s intercept the ball, the X1s leave the grid in the direction they were attacking and group behind the other teams to await another chance to enter the grid. If the ball is intercepted, the X2s move on attack against the X3s, who have entered the grid to defend. If a goal is scored, the X2s also leave the grid and group behind the teams behind the opposite goal. A new team, the X4s, from behind the goal scored upon becomes the attacker and moves on the opposite goal against the X3s. The game continues in this fashion for a set time or until each team has had two or more opportunities in the grid. The team scoring the most goals wins.

Variations:

1. Play 2 v 2 games.
2. Increase the size of the grid.

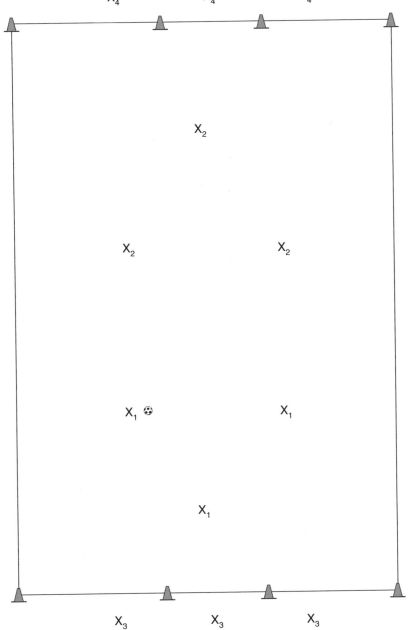

Two-Grid Possession

Contributor: B. Todd Dyer, Longwood College

Emphasis: Possession

No. of Players: 8

Equipment Needed: 1 ball, 6 cones, 8 practice jerseys

Setup: The game is played in an area 10 yards wide by 20 yards long, which is divided in half forming adjacent 10-by-10-yard grids. Six cones mark the corners and midfield of the grids. There are two teams of four players each, wearing different-colored practice jerseys. Each team has its own possession grid. One team, with a ball, is positioned within its possession grid. Two players from the other team are also within this grid, and the other two players are in their own grid.

Directions: The team in possession of the ball, using two-touch passing, tries to maintain possession of the ball in its grid while the two opponents try to gain possession of the ball. If the opponents gain possession, they are to pass or dribble the ball to their grid where their two teammates are waiting. Two players from the team that lost possession must sprint to the other grid and defend until they regain possession and get the ball back to their grid. Play is continuous with a 4 v 2 possession game played in either grid. Each time a team completes 10 consecutive passes it scores one point. The team with the most points after a predetermined time is the winner.

Variations: To vary difficulty of the game the coach may do the following:

1. Increase or decrease size of grids.
2. Increase or decrease number of players.
3. Limit teams to one-touch passing or allow unlimited touches.
4. Increase or decrease number of consecutive passes needed for a point.

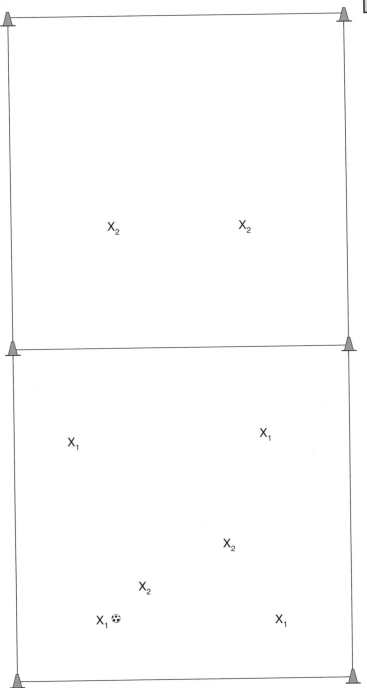

Contributor: Michael Alosco, Manhattan College

Emphases: Fitness, communication, heading

No. of Players: 22

Equipment Needed: 1 ball, 2 goals, 22 practice jerseys

Setup: The game is played in a regulation soccer field using four-foot high by six-foot wide goals. Two teams of 11 players each are positioned within each team's respective half of the field. The teams wear different-colored practice jerseys. A coach, with a ball, and one player from each team, X1 and X2, are in the midfield center circle. A goalkeeper is in each goal.

Directions: The game begins with a basketball jump ball toss by the coach between X1 and X2. The field players may use only their hands or heads. The goalkeepers may use only their hands or feet. The team that gains possession tries to move on goal by the player with the ball running with it or passing it to teammates. The defenders try to *tackle* the player with the ball by touching that player with two hands. When this occurs, the coach signals play to stop. The player who made the tackle is given the ball and allowed a free pass to a teammate to restart play. Scoring may occur only when one player passes to a teammate who heads the ball past the goalkeeper. Following a goal, the team scored upon restarts play with a free pass from the midfield center circle. Play is continuous for 20 minutes. The team with the most goals wins.

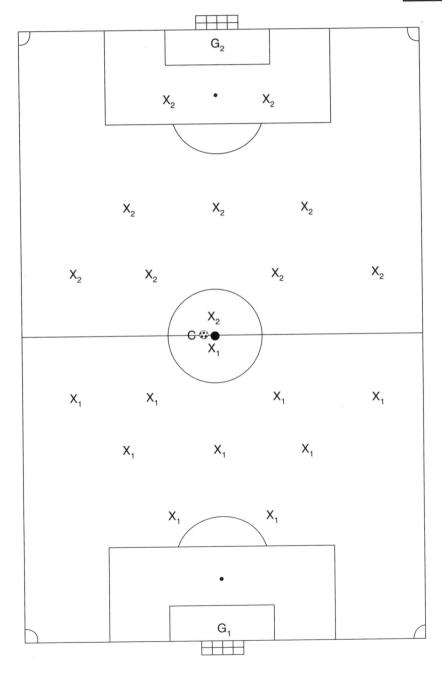

Ultimate Three Versus Three

Contributor: Colleen M. Hacker, Pacific Lutheran University

Emphases: Attack, defense, transition play

No. of Players: 11

Equipment Needed: 5 balls, 4 cones, 2 goals, 9 practice jerseys

Setup: The game is played in an area 40 yards long by 25 yards wide bordered by a cone at each corner. A goal is at the midpoint of each end line. Three teams of three players each wear different-colored practice jerseys. Two teams, X1 and X2, are positioned in opposite halves of the area. A player on X1 has a ball. The third team, X3, stands outside the area at midfield. A goalkeeper is in each goal. Two extra balls are in each goal.

Directions: The X1 player with the ball begins 3 v 3 play with a pass to a teammate. The game continues until one team scores two goals. Each time a team scores, it gets the ball back from the goalkeeper scored upon and attacks the opposite goal. The moment one team scores its second goal, the losing team runs off the field. The sideline team runs on the field to defend against the winning team, which has immediately attacked the opposite goal. Play is continuous for a predetermined time. The team scoring the most goals wins.

Variations:

1. Vary the field size according to skill levels.
2. Vary the number of players.
3. Vary the number of goals needed to win (one or three instead of two).

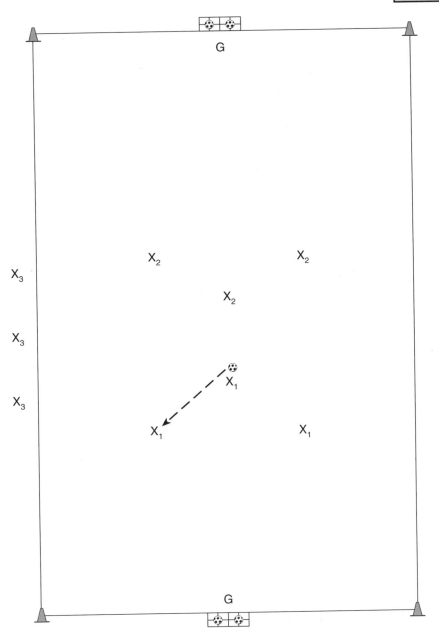

Zone Times Three

Contributor: Tracey Ranieri, SUNY at Oneonta

Emphasis: Attack

No. of Players: 14

Equipment Needed: 1 ball, 8 cones, 2 goals, 12 practice jerseys

Setup: An area 75 yards long by 50 yards wide is divided into three zones of 25 yards by 50 yards marked by cones. The middle zone is designated the neutral zone. A goal is at the midpoint of each end of the area. There are three teams of four players each, wearing different-colored practice jerseys. Each team is positioned within a different zone. A goalkeeper is in each goal. A player on the team in the neutral zone has a ball.

Directions: Team X2 in the neutral zone begins play by moving into Zone 1 and attempting to score against the X1s. If the X1s gain possession of the ball, they may carry it into the neutral zone. Only the team in possession of the ball may enter the neutral zone. The X1s then move into Zone 3 and attempt to score against the X3s. Any ball recovered by the goalkeeper is played to the team on defense, which then carries the ball into the neutral zone and on to the next zone to attack the team in that zone. Regulation rules are followed on all violations and out-of-bounds balls. Play is continuous until a goal is scored. The team scoring restarts play from the neutral zone toward the opposite goal. The team with the most goals after a predetermined time is the winner.

Variations:

1. Increase or decrease the number of players or size of playing area.

2. Limit play to two or one touch.

3. Require specific combination plays before shooting on goal.

4. Add neutral players in Zones 1 and 3 who serve as extra attackers.

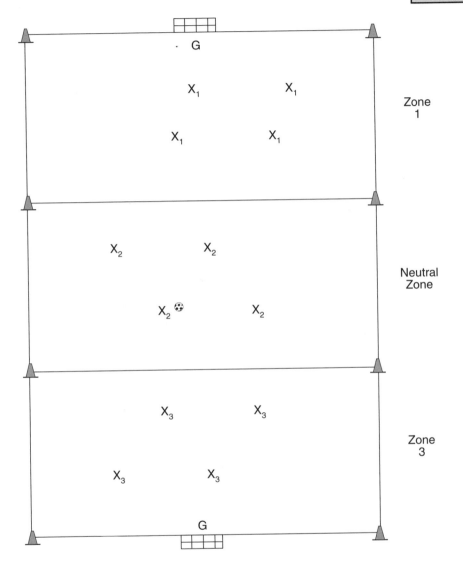

ABOUT THE EDITORS

J. Malcolm Simon

John A. Reeves

Malcolm Simon and John Reeves combine more than 50 years of coaching expertise in their newest coaching guide, *Practice Games for Winning Soccer*. Simon and Reeves are the editors of four other highly acclaimed Human Kinetics soccer books: *Soccer Restart Plays, Select Soccer Drills, The Soccer Games Book, and The Coaches Collection of Soccer Drills*.

Malcolm Simon is professor and director emeritus of physical education and athletics at the New Jersey Institute of Technology (NJIT). He has coached soccer, basketball, tennis, and volleyball in college, camp, and YMCA settings since 1954. His teams include National Association of Intercollegiate Athletics (NAIA) national champions and runners-up. Sixteen of his players have been named All-Americans and five have gone on to play professional soccer nationally and internationally. Upon his retirement in 1994, Simon was awarded the Allan R. Cullimore Medal for Distinguished Service by NJIT.

Twice the Conference Coach of the Year and twice the New Jersey College Coach of the Year, **John Reeves** achieved a remarkable 172-84-28 record in his 20 years as a collegiate soccer coach, leading his teams to three conference championships. He created and directed two extremely successful summer soccer schools, one at Drew University and one at the University of Rochester; both serve hundreds of youngsters each summer. A past president of the Intercollegiate Soccer Association of America (ISAA), Reeves is currently the director of athletics and physical education at Columbia University, where he earned his doctoral degree in 1983. He is a member of the National Soccer Coaches Association of America (NSCAA).

Simon and Reeves were inducted into the New Jersey Soccer Coaches Association Hall of Fame in 1995.

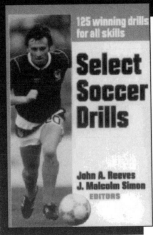
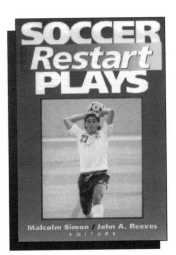

TRAINING GUIDES FOR FIRST-CLASS PLAY

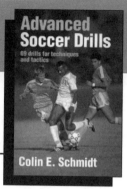

Advanced Soccer Drills
Colin E. Schmidt
1997 • Paper • 176 pp • Item PSCHO614
ISBN 0-88011-614-5 • $14.95 ($21.95 Canadian)

69 drills for techniques and tactics

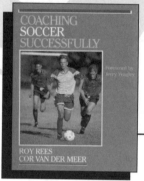

Coaching Soccer Successfully
Roy Rees and Cor van der Meer
Foreword by Jerry Yeagley
1997 • Paper • 240 pp • Item PREEO444
ISBN 0-87322-444-2 • $18.95 ($27.95 Canadian)

Techniques, tactics, and teambuilding

High-Performance Soccer
Techniques and Tactics for Advanced Play
Paul Caligiuri with Dan Herbst
Foreword by Cobi Jones
1997 • Paper • 256 pp • Item PCALO552
ISBN 0-88011-552-1 • $14.95 ($21.95 Canadian)

A World Cup veteran shares the secrets to success

Skills and Strategies for Coaching Soccer
Alan Hargreaves
1990 • Paper • 384 pp • Item PHARO328
ISBN 0-88011-328-6 • $19.95 ($29.95 Canadian)

Field-tested methods for developing top-notch soccer players

Human Kinetics
The Premier Publisher for Sports & Fitness
http://www.humankinetics.com/

Prices subject to change.